Remembering the Future

The Physics of the Soul
and
Time Travel

Written by Brooks A. Agnew
Illustrations by Brooks A. Agnew

iUniverse, Inc.
New York   Bloomington

Remembering the Future
The Physics of the Soul and Time Travel

iUniverse books may be ordered through booksellers or by contacting:

iUniverse
1663 Liberty Drive
Bloomington, IN 47403
www.iuniverse.com
1-800-Authors (1-800-288-4677)

Because of the dynamic nature of the Internet, any Web addresses or links contained in this book may have changed since publication and may no longer be valid. The views expressed in this work are solely those of the author and do not necessarily reflect the views of the publisher, and the publisher hereby disclaims any responsibility for them.

ISBN: 978-1-4502-5248-5 (pbk)
ISBN: 978-1-4502-5250-8 (cloth)
ISBN: 978-1-4502-5249-2 (ebk)

Printed in the United States of America

iUniverse rev. date: 9/2/2010

Table of Contents

This book is dedicated to the Queen.

Introduction

I have always been fascinated with time travel. I watched *The Time Tunnel* when I was young, and I was enthralled with *The Terminator* not so much for the syncopated music or the special effects, but because of the time paradox of John Connors' parent coming back in time to father the idol he would follow in the future. It was the reason I watched it so many times. In fact, I thought about the circle of cause and effect thousands of times since. I decided that everything we do will eventually affect the universe, and that I should be about doing it on purpose

When I began my graduate work in Physics, I became fascinated and frustrated with the Observation Effect. The realization that no matter how careful I was, even with passive observations, the sample measurement was never consistent. There was always an error and standard deviation that could not be explained. In frustration with my experimental results in developing laminated photopolymers, I penned in the body of my lab notebook one day, "The secret to life is clean glassware and conversion factors," that was of such amusement to my professor that he gave the only "A" that year to me.

Then, a book came out that carried with it enough buzz that I could not help but by it. It was called *The Secret*

Rhonda Byrne hit on something in that book. The relation of tiny causes, such as intention, to a much larger landscape of effects called reality was the ultimate test of resonance theory. I bought a healthy supply of refrigerator magnets and a pair of scissors and went to work. Before long I had converted my appliance into a veritable intention machine. It took a while before I noticed something happen. Nothing.

I then bought the film and watched it as well. Perhaps I missed something. I added some more universe channels to my design. Still the results purported by kings and historical figures throughout the ages did not materialize. Like the time paradox in the movies, I was hooked on thinking about it. The premise that we are in charge of our own life condition was now solid in my mind. I just didn't like my life condition. I figured there were millions of people with the same disappointment in the way things were turning out. The evidence that *Inc Magazine* mentioned that 16% of people include winning the Lottery as part of their retirement strategy fortified my desire to find out more about this Law of Attraction.

I knew Rhonda had really found something, but there was also something missing. I was an engineer and a scientist accustomed to tackling new situations and problems, so I began working through the problem. Like any challenge for which there are no formulas, no handbooks, and no instruction manual everything had to be done from scratch. I was convinced that the Law of Attraction was not fully derived, that is to say the proof lacked a few steps. Like building a geometric proof – you remember Sophomore Geometry don't you? – I needed to discover the axioms and postulates it would take to activate the Law and make it produce results. People needed a way to jump from where they perceive they are in life to their dream job or their optimum life condition.

In my interviews to gather information for this book, I found thousands of people who had read *The Secret* as well, and they came away with similarly unfulfilled dreams. At first, they didn't want to admit they had even bought the magnets for their refrigerators. And, like the Emperor's new clothes lauded by the icons of daytime television and late night telethons, they didn't want to comment on the nudity of the idea.

Then, one night while preparing an exam for my math students taking college algebra, some of whom had never solved a fraction before, I found the answer. The application of resonance, Fibonacci sequencing, and chaos theory blew me off my chair. I worked for months correlating it to the Law of Attraction completing the proof. Rhonda had hit on something and all the people needed were the key to unlock *The Secret*. This book is that key.

This book is organized to lead you through the forest on a slightly lit path. I can't just drop you into the deep woods of quantum physics and fourth dimensional concepts with nothing but a pocket calculator and expect you to buy this book. Can I? So, you are going on the same journey I traveled. You will go back in time and forward in time and remember what you saw. And when you bring those memories back to the present, the resistance of your life to movement will yield to your intention. The law of Attraction will work for you as it did for me.

Preface

The Universe is the mathematical sum of the intentions of every sentient being in it. There are a little more than six billion realities alive on the Earth at the publishing of this book. In the year 2015, when I wrote this book, there are nearly 7.9 billion. Every one of them is perfect for the being who observes it. Regardless of whether sentient beings are conscious they are conscious or not, the formula cannot be usurped by any force. Not even God, or a whole host of gods, can change that. The free intention of any being is the charge and right of that being to exercise it to his or her will. Should God change the intention of a single sentient being, the entire universe would collapse. The consciousness that holds energy together to form matter would be destroyed forever; at least for this *eternity*.

After nearly thirty years of scientific research and engineering, I became highly trained in analyzing complex processes. Classically educated as a physicist in instrumental analysis, I learned to appreciate the nuances of the Observation Effect. As Nicolas Cage's character stated in the opening narration of the movie *Next*, "The future changes just because you looked at it."[1]

The purpose of this book is to awaken the reader to the idea that everything past, present and future can be affected by the intention of a single sentient being. The extent of that effect is as

---

[1] 27 April, 2007 Next: A Las Vegas magician who can see into the future is pursued by FBI agents seeking to use his abilities to prevent a nuclear terrorist attack.

variable as the number of sentients in the set of numbers and for each of us is different.

It isn't designed to bury you in math formulas, although I had to include some to more thoroughly explain some of the relationships. Although some controversial concepts, such as entangled particle theory, are added to show that we have a basis in physics for the Law of Attraction, I think you'll understand it just fine. There is an awakening of sorts taking place in the community of physicists around the world. The inclusion of consciousness in the transition of energy to matter is finally reaching the lectern, having finally made its way past the high priests of science. It is also included in this book as we are about to reveal a stunning mathematical tool that will finally unlock the secret of manifestation.

No two sentient beings are exactly the same, nor are their realities the same. Even twins and soul mates are different souls, and therefore not equal in their stimulus upon the universe. Of course, should millions or even billions of sentient beings, such as humans for instance, apply their intention in a focused and coordinated manner, there is absolutely no limit to what could be created, or, for that matter, destroyed. The more sentient beings that are added to the set, the more stable the population becomes. That is to say, unless members of that population become self aware and empowered to rock the boat a little.

One thing must be made absolutely clear. The beings of Earth, whether they were born here or are just visitors, have a choice and a responsibility. Don't think for another moment you have to march

7

inexorably down the path of eschatology to Armageddon. When you are done with this book, you will all realize that we can all choose a new path to a world far away from the woes of the prophets. There is no blasphemy in this, I can assure you. The very prophecies given to us were warnings as to what *would* happen *if* we did not change our ways. Nothing in the Scriptures says there is no way we cannot get out of this alive. On the contrary, not only can we get out of this alive with all of our memories and accomplishments, we can also live while we are here. We are one hundred percent responsible for our own life condition.

I taught advanced Biblical scholars for more than 30 years and faced every conceivable argument for the points made in this book. They hold true and have passed the test.

There are thousands of "self-help" books on the market. They may each have their merits. You want the tools you need to personally stop the cycle of failure in your life and move toward success. Don't you? I'll try to bring this to you as easily as I can, but there is not much time.

Some of this is complicated to explain. That's why other self-help books haven't been what you're looking for. This book will give you tools and revelations that are true and powerful in learning to work the Law of Attraction. The contents of this book are still considered paranormal in this day. That's why I am uniquely qualified to write this book. It required a single mind of a physicist, a statistician, a mathematician, and a writer who can tell the story to the average person. It also required a discovery of how, out of the chaotic universe, order and beauty arises beyond description. You will receive the benefits of my discovery in this book.

There is a need for enlightened and awakened people producing positive energy and success. The world needs thousands of you. Millions would be better. In here, you will learn how to access and thus affect your life energy with purpose and direction and when to make the move.

You will also learn about the tool of *clearing*. When a person fails at something, they often say, "I will never do that again." Or they may declare, "I will never allow that to happen again." In fact, they have already sent out the energy to guarantee that they will in fact do it again and again. They may proceed in business, or love, or in any sort of pursuit of happiness to the same place and fail, over and over again. Most people will say something like, "Well the powers that *be* just don't want me to have that." Another favorite I hear is, "If it is meant to be, then I guess I'll be successful. If it is not meant to be, then I guess I won't." The notion that the universe has a destiny for each person, a sort of teleology from which they are powerless to deviate, has been the ploy of governments and religions since the dawn of time. It is also categorically false.

This book may also bring to your remembrance – I hesitated to use the word *discovery*, because you already knew this – that you are an eternal being having a mortal experience. You are not the calcium and protein filled with water that warms your bicycle seat. You may have been born like most mammals, spewing amniotic fluid, gasping for air, and reeling from the cold shock of evaporation against your skin. You may feel your world as a cold or hot thing of pleasure or pain through the billions of electrical sensors on your skin. You may experience your environment like a chaotic smoothie poured into your head through delicately designed tympanic stereo. But it isn't like that at all. The nano-world that fits into a mere three dimensions is only a comma in a twenty-four-volume set of instruction manuals for reality.

The being that makes up the person you *are*, is only temporarily occupying solid matter in the form of your physical body. The real *you* is older than you can imagine. In fact, the entire universe is folded up inside of each and every human soul in the universe. It is a total agreement between every sentient being in the universe. If one sentient being were to leave this universe, the entire composition would collapse back into the void and have to start all over again with a new total set of intelligences in agreement.

You will learn in this book that the Big Bang never happened. The universe is still a singularity with all the matter, both seen and unseen, stilled packed into zero distance and zero time. You must realize before you lay this book down that you are *Source*. You are a particle of God. You must not believe for another moment that you are separate from source. God you were, and God you always will be. Not to rule or lord over the masses, but to serve. Religions have been working since the dawn of civilization to build and control congregations by telling people that they cannot get to heaven unless they are members in good standing of their religion. They sing about love, but they preach one universal message: fear.

Fear is around forty times more powerful than love at manifesting the future. A young mother who had terminal cancer approached a dear friend of mine who is a Catholic priest. She was bewildered as to why she was going to die. It wasn't fair. She had prayed every day since she was a little girl, after her mother died of cancer, that she would not get cancer. With kindness of an absolute saint, he said, "My God, woman. I would be completely shocked if you had lived your life thus far without getting cancer. You manifested it with your own fear."

The universe does not discriminate. It cannot. The program has rules in order to exist, and this is a rule. Whatever energy is sent out to the universe from a sentient being will vibrate everything that will sympathize with that energy. If you send fear out into the universe, then products of fear are what you may reap. If you send out products of love, then that is what you may reap.

One word of great advice here. It does not matter how *you* are loved by others. It only matters how you love *them*. Do not be surprised if you aren't loved by everyone. Even Jesus had enemies. In order for you to work the Law of Attraction to its fullest positive effect, you are strongly advised to master loving everyone, beginning with yourself. You must love yourself. You will learn more about this further along in the book.

You have eons of experience. And that means you may have learned many things through those experiences over countless mortalities of one kind or another and have forgotten them. Although all experiences are for a person's expansion and growth, they can also

11

establish patterns or habits or *scripts* that form blockages in the flow of energy. This simple principle was written into every scripture in the world, and then steadily and nearly completely erased from every page. Eternity doesn't start when you die. The truth is that it already started, and we're probably somewhere in the middle of it. Without the threat of eternal death, would anyone voluntarily surrender their sovereignty to a priest or a pastor?

The construction of these blockages or mirrors is done by the individual. They form an echo wall that short-circuits a person's Life Force over and over again. The presence of these wall surfaces acts like a mirror, reflecting the life energy instead of letting it flow through to fulfill the person's dream.

When conducted by a clearing practitioner, *clearing* is effective at removing these blockages or mirrors. That means the obstacles to the flow of life energy can be skillfully identified and removed forever. Although people may profess to do *clearing* in one workshop or another for groups of people, *clearing* is a one-on-one process during which people are changed forever. There is no "workshop high" that wears off a week or two after the event is completed. *Clearing* is a permanent life-change.

When a person's life energy is allowed to flow freely, his or her intentions can be fully empowered. The intentions of a human being are the most powerful creative forces in the universe. In fact, they *are* the creative forces in the universe. That means if you ever wondered about the identity of the creator, take some serious time and look in the mirror. Look into your own soul.

Manifestation is the literal creation process of a human soul. Each soul has all the potential and tools of godhood built into it. One of the most important things a person has to do is remember who they are, and that their potential is absolutely unlimited. Then, that person needs the toolbox to do the work of creation. That is what this book is about.

Millions of people were convinced the Law of Attraction was functional throughout the universe and would apply to anything they wished to accomplish. What they lacked were the tools to meet the conditions of the law. They put their pictures up on their refrigerator doors. They dreamed and hope and wished and cried, but not enough energy could be mustered to turn the planet. This is why I wrote this book and brought it back to the year 2010. The provision of these tools, along with the desire of millions of souls to reap the wealth of the universe, will be enough to redirect mankind away from where it is now in the year 2015. I can't give you all the details, but believe me when I tell you it is vital to the condition of Earth that the planet achieves a critical mass of *cleared* and functional souls at the *empowerment level* for Earth to survive.

With the momentum that swelled in the year 2010 with *The Secret* marketing effort, I strongly felt it was necessary to move our start date back to that year. If a message of awareness could be constructed in the past, utilizing the momentum of *The Secret*, I felt it was possible to empower enough human beings in time to avoid the events prior to the year 2015.

You are about to take a journey. It's the same journey I took. In traveling with me, you will be able to see how detailed you can see the past and the future. And I don't mean just the past of this current mortality. I also don't mean a single future. When you open up to potential of all potentialities, you may see just where you fit in the best.

When you finish the book, you will have learned how to visit future and the past, remember what you envisioned, and bring back that information to the past, which is the present to. That ability will change the direction of your life, and thus the course of planet Earth.

Read and grow, friends. We need you.

Brooks A. Agnew

Chiming winds,
Fragrant flame flowers,
Ocean's view,
And warm yellow stone;
Of home long since swallowed
In red Sun's cycle
Toward sleep;
I woke up here.

Chapter 1: Home World

Eight years ago, I was approached by a woman after I had completed a lecture on the speed of light and asked if I would like to co-author a book with her on the creation of the Earth. Curious, I admitted that the subject was irresistible and that I was a skeptical student and longtime teacher of the traditional religious stories we had heard our entire lives. Somehow the words, "…and the morning and the evening were the third day…" had a myriad of meanings flow through my mind each time I read them. It had nothing to do with my level of faith. It's just that the word *day* could mean anything from twenty-four hours to ten million years.

After all, the Earth didn't even receive a sun or moon until the third day according to the Biblical creation story, so how could there be *days* in the traditional sense of the word? The physics community is populated with various metaphysical theorists ever extrapolating and interpolating in attempts to understand how the universe was created. At the time, the distance physicists forayed into metaphysics was inversely proportional to one's ability to obtain tenure or obtain funding for research. But as the years progressed, more and more main-stream physicists were publishing papers on time travel, wormholes, and the functionality of multiple dimensions. This was a rare opportunity to be involved in a major publication about the subject. I had no idea it would end up being more than 1,500 pages of world-class research publication titled *The Ark of Millions of Years: Volumes I, II, and III* becoming a best seller. (www.arkofmillionsofyears.com)

She handed me a hand-written outline of her ideas for the book and gestured with her hands the gaps where she hoped I would inject the scientific aspects of her somewhat controversial archaeological approach to the subject. I agreed to proceed and began writing some chapters on dimensions and methods for considering the stability and practicality of super-massive spinning black holes serving as wormholes or star gates through which planets might move unharmed. We visited the Museum of Anthropology in Mexico City and found numerous ancient carvings, codices, and pieces of art that actually did a very good job of describing the possibility that Earth was not from around here. I quickly came up against the leading edge of known physics and had to search deeper in my mind for answers. I decided to revive a skill I had learned many years before. The ability quiet the mind enough to hear the echo of pasts and futures was necessary to connect the dots.

At eighteen, I was an airman in the Air Force stationed in Grand forks, North Dakota. It was springtime. The urge to meditate became overpowering, yet I had no training in doing so. Fortuitously, there was a teacher of Transcendental Meditation offering classes at the local University at night. I enrolled in earnest and started to connect with the quiet mind.

The mantra I received was simple and easy to repeat. My teacher appeared to be impressed that I could reach deep states of calmness in just a few minutes. I was able to disconnect myself from the stress that had bothered me as a youth and focus my learning ability. The groundwork for my lifetime of study and learning began by taking college classes in Humanities and Sociology on my own at night while pouring through the correspondence courses offered by the Air Force in Electronics Engineering.

Though I was able to calm my fleeting attention, there was something missing. I began to shape the process to meet my needs and found that I developed a sort of launching spot in my meditation state. It was a mountain meadow with tall green grass with a single white garden chair. The sky was often blue, and I could hear the wind singing through the trees like distant applause blending into one harmonious white noise. From there I could travel, as it were, to distant places and times. It was a good method of escape from the world and its pressures and feints within feints, which are desperately difficult to negotiate for a post-adolescent boy lacking parents. But, escape is not what I needed or wanted.

In my fifty-first year, I learned a new type of meditation, called Flower of Life, or MerKaBa meditation. It was then that the childhood dreams returned. It was like a distant memory. This was completely different then the Transcendental Meditation experience. And there was something else. I really don't know how the switch was turned on, but when the lights came on, it was like a whole chapter lost in my youth came into view very clearly.

The meditation structure will be discussed later in the book, so for now I want to explain the connections that were made, and the understanding that began to flow forth into my life. It will be significant for you as well, as I explain how this unfolded.

I learned to work the MerKaBa fields around me very well and very quickly, like a bird to flight. Shortly after my certification classes, something very powerful occurred. I had built a rather large spiral of energy above my body using the MerKaBa field that I learned to operate. I was lying on my back on a table in the center of 6 people standing around the table. The energy field went out of my heart area and about 20 meters straight up. When I got it up and stable, I collapsed it and shot the energy out of my arms and hands, which were at my sides on the table. About 2 hours later I came out of this, and one of the less sensitive bystanders, named Todd, said, "What was that energy pulse about?" He admitted he was a spiritual brick, when it came to sensing things, but even *he* felt the energy. But in the meantime, I want to continue telling you this experience, because it's extremely important.

All of a sudden, the meditation launching place changed. Without warning, I went into meditation expecting to see the warm sunny meadow with the clear blue skies before me. Much to my amazement, the following place came clearly into view as I entered my heart.

I was standing on a terrace of sorts. Looking down I could see the pale yellow patio stone polished and laid into place with a gray grouting, flat and smooth and warm. The terrace was about 10 meters across with a couple of odd angles at the edges from which was laid a short wall that was capped with the same yellow stones speckled with tiny gray veins. The capped wall formed a short bench all around the terrace, except where the short wall had an opening allowing people to enter the terrace from the house. The place was on the edge of a very high bluff of a fjord overlooking the sea to the left.

Fig 1. The terrace in the early days of construction, before the lattice was complete and the vines were planted.

The terrace had an open trestle made of dark wood overhead through which a green vine weaved itself populated with large pink and orange blossoms. The slats were lying on their edge about 30 centimeters apart. Each one was smooth and shiny and about 50 millimeters thick and about 20 centimeters tall. They each spanned the entire terrace and rested upon a beam of mirror-smooth dark wood with the most incredible grain that showed through the glossy polished face. These beams were about 50 centimeters tall and 10 centimeters thick. Each of the four corner posts were about 4 meters tall and equally stunning in appearance. The corners were perfect, with no twists or knots in the wood.

Hanging from the trestle were three wind chimes of a most curious design. The largest one was about 20 centimeters in diameter and was about 3 meters long. The next one was about 15 centimeters in diameter and 2 meters long, and the last was about 10 centimeters in diameter and about 1 meter long. Their construction was nothing short of flawless. Like ebony instruments, they were smooth as ceramic pipes. The wood was black and grainless. The chime wall was about 8 millimeters thick and perfectly cylindrical. There was no evidence of machining, sawing, or sanding. The edges were rounded, not like one would see from a pipe that had been cut off with a saw. This wood was finely and perfectly shaped.

They were suspended from a wooden peg in the wood trestle with what looked like a thick hair coming down and splitting into three parts about 30 centimeters from the top of each chime and passing through three small holes equidistant in the circumference of the edge, just below the round rim. The hair was deftly tied with the same knot tightly done as though part of the art of the construction.

The striking mechanism for each chime was most interesting. They each had a ratcheting wheel with a cog attached to a dried hard leaf paddle that flapped gently in the ocean breeze. The leaves were each the same size and a beautiful golden brown, shaped like a heart and so thin that the veins of its previously green life were clearly visible. They were identically curved with the stem lashed tightly to a wooden dowel that was attached to a ratchet on a wooden wheel with 12 steps carved into its 20 centimeter circumference. As the paddle waved in the cool and gentle ocean breeze, a tightly-wound animal skin mallet would ratchet up higher and higher until it would release at after the 12th step and would strike the chime. Each mechanism was separate and mounted on the terrace wall at a height that would allow the mallet to strike the chime in the exact center of its length. The random dropping of the mallets created a non-rhythmic and perfectly tuned harmony that was peaceful and musical. Depending on which chime was most recently struck, the accent would shift from high to low. The music seemed to join the scent of the fluorescently live flowers that populated the trestle overhead.

The sky above the sea was the most amazing sight. In the morning, the sun would rise red and cool. It was so large it filled nearly the entire horizon. After about 6 hours, the sun would clear the sea covering nearly the whole sky overhead. It was only partially solid. The center was about a third of the diameter. Its corona was round with ejections licking out into space like swirling pink steam frozen in almost imperceptible wafts. Surrounding the sun, clearly visible through the translucent corona, two stars twinkled to the South brightly. Two large planets faintly drifted across the sky to the North. The larger of the two was a deep-water blue and the other nearly blood red.

This was the launching place into which I awakened each time I drifted into my Earthly MerKaBa meditations. MerKaBa mediation will be explained later in this book. This was my heart place. The peace and tranquility that I enjoyed became welcome solace from a

21

physical world that often did not feel like home. Over the years, it was difficult to tell the difference between worlds. That is to say, the noise and strife of Earth was a sharp contrast to the solitude of this terrace view. I memorized its moods and colors. The atmosphere enveloped me like a lover. And one day, after what seemed like years of waking up in this place, I became aware of my last world and my life bejeweled with the treasures I describe herein.

The emotions I had already experienced in these MerKaBa-enabled memories often overwhelmed me. It was only preparation for what I discovered in this distant and yet local heart-world. In a moment I can only equate to that of an infant who discovers for the first time his own feet and hands, I looked down at my own hands. They were golden brown and smooth like they were new. There was not a blemish or a flaw. The five fingers and one thumb were long with four joints in each. They were thin and muscular. The palms were smooth and narrow. I recall looking at them for hours, amazed at their perfection and beauty. My wrists were thin and smooth, coming from a light brown shirt sleeve with no cuff. Rather, it was a finely woven fabric that felt like thick silk and yet was warm on the skin.

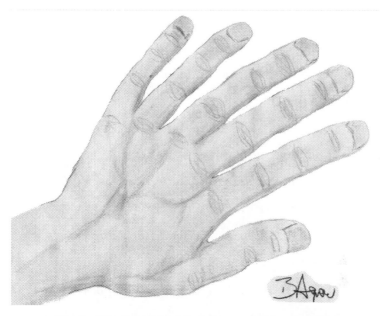

Fig 2. The hand had five fingers and a thumb.

In this experience of awareness, I felt of my face, which was often wet with my tears of joy of the scent, sounds, and view from my wonderful terrace. My skin was smooth, without hair or stubble like my face on Earth. In a moment like stepping to edge of a cliff with wings for the first time, I leaned forward to peer into the polished yellow capstone of the terrace wall. The beautiful realization of my own face still takes my breath as I recall the experience.

My jaw line was thin, with little depth from the lower lip to the square chin. My lips were full and could smile widely, with a shape that I memorized over the years. They were expressive and graceful, and yet noble and curved so as to convey a peaceful greeting. My large oval eyes were the color of the aqua sea, with no whites, and the black pupil was equally and concentrically oval in shape with the longer distance from side-to-side. The lids were high under the brow, which was drawn with a thick line of short golden hair. The forehead was tall and wider than the cheekbones, which were round above dimpled cheeks slightly drawn and graceful down to the chin. My hair was shoulder length, straight and thick. It was shiny and golden like metal, and yet it flowed and spilled like water over my light brown shirt loosely cut around the neck. My neck was long. Very long. My head could turn nearly 180 degrees as there were two extra vertebrae than my Earth body.

I was two and a half meters tall, mostly from the two extra vertebrae in the neck and the long leg bones. I had two rows of teeth on the sides and one row across the front. The front teeth were square on the bottom and white as snow. The pallet was high and when I touched it with my tongue; I could feel the smoothness of it. The nose was long and straight with somewhat flaring nostrils and a thin square tip.

Waking up here

There is one more thing, before I continue to describe my home. I don't know when or how I first made a sound with my voice. On Earth, during my entire life from my earliest youth to this day, I have spoken in my sleep. The language is clear and complex with beautiful tones and words that sound like something out of heaven itself. It is also undecipherable by anyone who has ever heard it. On Earth, I recall being often awakened by my mother when I was nine years old after my complaining younger sister, attempting sleep in the room down the hall, demanded she do so to make me stop talking.

"Stop talking gibberish," she would scold. "You're keeping everyone awake. Who are you talking to anyway?" she would ask sternly.

Now, I have to explain something. There is no proper place to tell this, so here and now is as good a time as any in this book. I have only told this story to a very few and select persons in my mortal life. My fingers tremble even now as I seek the keys to make these words. It isn't as though I trust you. But there isn't much time for you, so I am risking my private soul to make sure you understand the truth of what I am about to tell you. Put your dogma aside. Lay down your prejudice. Prepare yourself with an open heart to read the most private and sovereign words I have ever penned.

My younger sister was born with cystic fibrosis, from which she finally died at the age of twelve. Her youth was fraught with visits to hospitals and specialists, and yet in my youth I was kept separated from this experience. While my father would take her to Albuquerque, New Mexico for treatments of some kind or another, my mother and her parents would take me camping in High Sierras. They weren't an outdoors type of people. We lived in a fine house in southern California with marble floors and foreign antiques. As though they were answering some kind of mission call, each summer they would load a tent and one fishing pole with some basic tackle into the Ford Falcon wagon and head across the desert hours before the scorching Sun would preclude such a trip. I remember sitting in the back seat with a wool blanket over my legs in the predawn chill with the hum of the tires blazing across the pavement at forty-five miles an hour for hours and hours, until the mountains would appear in the distant

25

desert haze. I don't remember any of the actual camping experiences, except one.

In the summer of my ninth year on Earth, we arrived at the campsite. It was a well-kept area with parking for one vehicle at each campsite. There was a water spigot at each campsite, but no electricity, and a picnic table. We pitched two olive green army surplus tents. The first day we had a late lunch and played some cards. Time doesn't seem to mean much at that age, and I was a solitary child with what would be diagnosed these days as Attention Deficit Syndrome. I bounced from one thought to another like ten movies playing at the same time inside my head. Night came and with it a warm sleeping bag inside the larger tent.

I remember waking up and crawling out of the tent to walk down to the cinder block bathroom facility. When I came back, the family was still waking up. I got my tackle box together and my fishing pole. In the High Sierras, there is always a trout stream somewhere nearby. Such was the case with this campsite. I don't remember if I ate breakfast or not. One of the symptoms of my mental state at that age was a lack of appetite. I recall countless visits with my mother to one doctor or another for some sort of elixir that would make me eat. "Take another bite," I would hear my mother incessantly say. I was always the last to leave the table. I developed incredible skills at hiding tomatoes until I could dispose of them somewhere. I still to this day will not eat a raw tomato. I am sure you had those *acquired-taste* foods forced upon you as well. After all, life can't be filled with chocolate ice cream and pizza.

As my grandfather poked his head out of the tent, no doubt headed for the blockhouse, I said, "I'm going fishing," and motioned to the sound of gurgling water about sixty meters from our campsite. I walked with my pole and tackle box down the gravel road and onto the pathway worn by numberless anglers who had gone before me.

Stream fishing was more like casting practice for me. I don't recall ever catching a fish from a stream. I do recall one Summer Lake fishing with my older half-brother, nine years my senior, and my grandfather. We were in an aluminum boat in a lake on Mount Palomar. I caught twenty-five fish. They caught none. They moved me from one end to another and then to the middle. We were all using the same worms. They even switched poles with me. "I hear a fish," I would say. Then I would haul another one to the surface. They never took me fishing again.

This morning, something happened that changed my life, and theirs, forever. I remember the stream. It was powerful and swirling, flowing around a large rock with a voice that sounded wonderful. It was calming and seemed to ebb the unfinished thoughts in my head. I cast into a deep pool that eddied peacefully in the shadow of a large rock. I didn't hear a fish. In fact, I don't remember casting a second time.

The next thing I remember, I was walking the return path back toward the campsite after what seemed like only a few minutes of casting practice, which would have been typical for my habit of incompleting anything or any thought of any kind. I hadn't caught a thing. I rejoined the gravel road and continued to walk toward the campsite.

But instead of finding the lone campers, as the rest of the camping park was deserted, I found a flurry of activity. The ranger's mint green jeep was there with the yellow light flashing on top. My mother was standing there in front of him with her arms folded yelling. Again. She yelled a lot. When I drew within 40 meters or so, they turned toward me. All of them. I felt like I was late to class, again. I was in trouble. I was very familiar with this energy.

"Where the hell have you been?" my mother yelled.

I wasn't a screamer, so I kept walking before I spoke. "I was fishing right up there," pointing to the stream over the hill and down the well-worn path.

"The hell you were," she spat. "We've been searching for you all day."

All day? All day? How could it have been all day? "I didn't catch anything. I was only there for a little while," I complained through tears that came so easily to me at this time in my life. My mind raced through a list of excuses that had worked in the past. I would like to have used any of them if I had to, in order to avoid another beating within an inch of my life. It was a common threat my mother used in what seemed like my middle name, as I recall. I neared the campsite with an overwhelming flinch building within me.

The ranger spoke up with a calm voice that offered the father-figure steadiness the entire situation demanded at this moment. I knew instantly there would be no beating today. Not this time. Not with him there. "Where did you go, son?"

"I was fishing right down by the big rock on the path," I responded without whining.

28

"We saw your tackle box and your pole, but you were nowhere to be found." Well, I might have thrown a few stones into the water. I might have looked for lizards. I might have looked at the clouds that often appeared out of nowhere in the High Sierras at eight thousand feet. "You were gone for nine hours."

"Huh?" I asked in complete disbelief. "That's impossible." This also was one my favorite responses. As though gnomes or fairies would slip in and mess everything up, I remember shaking my head in utter confusion as I got the blame for one disaster or another. That is, except for swinging on the gate. That whipping I got many times, simply because I loved swinging on the gate. That was me.

"Son, we have had every ranger on the mountain looking for you all day. I'm just glad you're safe." He shook my grandfather's hand, got back into his jeep, and drove away. Somewhere, a safety report would take hours to fill out.

Nine hours? Nine hours? How could that be? I was finally hungry, but I had no idea that much time had gone by. I don't remember anything more about that trip. I don't remember the trip home. I don't remember getting beaten or anything.

The coming school year was when I first noticed the change. I read everything. I mean everything. The SRA reader box must have had 200 short stories in it. They were ranked by grade level; yellow, green, blue and red in order of difficulty. At the end of each story booklet was a series of ten questions to answer. I read them all in a few weeks on my own. My teachers could not believe the change. My handwriting was acceptable. My math was perfect, although I stopped showing my work on paper. The answers came to me so quickly that I

29

blurted out the answers in class. My thoughts were clear and my mind worked like never before.

There was this one incident at home that I remember particularly well a few months after the *missing time* in the High Sierras. We had purchased a color TV the year before. It was a Zenith. We were one of the first people in our Long Beach neighborhood to own a color TV. It also didn't work well. The picture rolled vertically, and the picture quality was snowy. I decided to fix it.

I was alone in the house, which was typical for me. I unplugged the TV and removed the Masonite rear cover off the back of the TV set. I looked inside at all the tubes and wires. Without hesitation, I removed all the tubes from their sockets and put them into a cardboard box. I remembered an electronic store at the top of the hill on State Street in a small strip mall. I lifted some money from my mother's purse, also a typical activity for me, and loaded the box onto the handlebars of my bicycle. I remember arriving at the electronics store, where inside the door was a tube tester. It was the size of a stove, with dozens of sockets in it. One by one, I inserted the tube into the socket that had the right part number and had the right number of pin holes. I pressed the TEST button and watched the needle on the meter. The ones that indicated GOOD in the green zone I put back in the box. The ones that indicated BAD in the red zone, I placed on the counter.

When I was finished testing about 25 tubes from that TV set, I searched the shelves under the testing bench for the right part numbers that were printed in white on the side of each silvered glass tube. I found them all. I took the new ones to the register and paid for them. "Are you sure you know what you're doing?" asked the store manager. "Sure do," was my smiling reply.

When I returned to the house, my older half-brother was just coming in from college. He attended Long Beach State College only a few miles away. He drove a very nice red 1955 Chevy with three speeds on the column. He was also completely white-faced with fear because I had just walked into the house with a box full of tubes that came out of the family color TV set. Without any delay or explanation, I returned to the back of the TV and began reinstalling all the tubes.

Within a few minutes, the tubes were all in place, the back was reinstalled, and the cord was put back into the receptacle. I walked around the front, and pulled the volume control to the ON position. Perfect. The picture was perfect. My brother knew from that moment on, the world would never be the same.

Going back in

The house next to the terrace was dark brown, made from the wood obtained from the local forest. It was a single story with wooden floors and featured a winding, white stone walkway from the front door and terrace to the cobblestone road. The road was rather steep and yet easy to walk as the stones were flat and laid smoothly into the hard soil and led to a small village square lined with alabaster white buildings with dark brown window frames and a friendly open windows.

The community of small people had dark brown straight hair, large brown eyes, and a slightly olive skin. Barely a meter and a half

31

tall with slight shoulders and tiny hands, they were friendly and peaceful and simple. These people had evolved through millennia of growth and technological advancement. Their rich planet had been invaded by a conquering race from another world centuries ago. The word of the wealth of this world spread throughout the system, and yet another race arrived to wrestle for dominance. This race had conscripts that swelled its ranks of warriors. Some of the conscripts were experts at communication and negotiation. My people were among these conscripts.

My ancestors were used by the conquerors as forward scouts. They were very fast and capable of traveling more distance over any terrain than any ground vehicle. They had learned from experience not to enter a new world with more technology than was necessary to take over the infrastructure. Some race could capture and copy technology in a matter of weeks, but if they did not see high technology, they could not copy it. So they sent us in to discover the hearts of the people. Our empathic abilities gave us an unfair advantage. The hostages held on our home world kept the scouts in line. That is until the scouts were left for dead or abandoned in the field. They would often settle on those worlds and live long after the conquerors has gone home with their spoils.

This particular world was very high tech, when the conquerors arrived. They were mechano-biologists. They had learned to grow machines that were alive, and displayed levels of artificial intelligence with a priority on adaptation. Acting like an evolutionary survival instinct, these machines made it impossible for the conquerors to secure any area of the planet for very long. The costs of occupation were prohibitive, until they figured out how to make a virus to infect the machines. The viral attack left this planet of the red Sun without so much as a flying machine or weapon other than ancient projectile weapons.

With a completely independent power source for every biological device, there was never any major power distribution. By the time I was born, the only electricity was provided by using tree sap and sea water batteries as storage devices that chemically flowed mild current suitable for low-wattage lights made of bioluminescent bulbs made of stretched animal intestines and filled with an eternal algae. Although there were sufficient resources for more power, such as the left over hydrogen III stone mines, the people seemed to be very satisfied with the comforting labors that were necessary to get through a normal day.

In fact, there was no monetary system. People simply worked at what they loved doing, and did it for the love of their hearts for one another. When I wanted a hard brown nut-bread roll, I went to the baker who always seemed to be bringing a flat ceramic pan of aromatic rolls out of his stone oven just as I arrived. They could not be bitten with the teeth off the roll. One would break the roll in the hands with a wringing motion, and then toss the smaller piece into the mouth. If it was not fresh, a quick swirl of water or hot cocoa would render it perfect for the pallet. They had a wonderful smoky cinnamon taste from the redwood nuts and a satisfying texture from the wheat flour, and were amazingly nutritious, especially with berry jam.

When the baker needed clothes, he simply went to the tailor who loved to make clothes and loved even more when people wore them into the village for all to see. When he needed his hair trimmed, the barber was ready with loving scissors in deft little hands. The same relationship applied for carpentry, plumbing, and every little trade in the world. There was so much love in the system that there was no need for laws of any kind. In most sentient societies, ninety-eight percent of the population obeys the laws as a matter of ethics. Two percent of the population commits nearly one hundred percent of the crimes, and it is the same crowd that will not obey the law. Police are commissioned in proper proportions to this level of crime. Armies are marshaled to either defend against national attacks, or to perpetrate attacks on other countries. In the case of this world, they neither had police nor armies when the conquerors came to reap the mineral bounties from this world. Without using force to overcome, the forceful will internally destroy themselves. This is what happened to them, and without the resolve to even return the conscripts to their homes, they left this planet when the Sun evolved into a red giant. The inflation of the wealth of this world hauled back to their own destroyed their economy. They never recovered, and they never returned.

The village children would come up the path in the evenings, which were long and lazy as the giant red sun would take hours upon hours to drop out of sight. Even then, the glowing light would reflect off the two planets in the sky and was augmented by the two bright stars which could be seen nearly all the time. The rotation of the planet had slowed so much, how long it took for a single revolution on its axis remained unpredictable. It seemed all the years I went there, and still do, that the sky scene remained much the same. The changes

34

that took place were subtle and evolutionary in nature. As the world grew cooler, the lifeforms changed, the birds' songs repopulated, and the smell of warm cocoa became even more attractive.

With the children visiting the fjord-side terrace, the wind chimes toning, the evenings eventually turned into song. First they would sing, and then my queen and I would sing.

Ah yes, the queen. She is a most amazing creature. Her hair, like mine, is long and light, coating the shoulders and back like silk. Her skin, like mine, was somewhat glittery and golden in color as though it was permanently tanned and sprinkled with very fine sparkles. Her skin was capable of *seeing*. That is to say, it was sensitive to energy in a wide range of frequencies. Another being's consciousness could be read like the colors of a painting. These frequencies often flowed and changed in color depending on the interaction or awareness of the being. It provided a power of discernment that allowed our race, of which we seemed to be the only two on this world left, to serve our citizens with counseling and leadership that was perfect and complete.

Fig 3. The Queen.

There was no guile or pretention or deception that could be kept from her. Beings walked in a pure state of transparency in front of her. There was no need to judge another for anything, as their own state of energy was their judgment. Our service was simply that of facilitating the higher frequencies to blossom and flow with joy whenever they could do so.

The children's songs were always unique. Human children like to hear the same song or see the same movie over and over again. It is a form of security, for in their minds they know what is coming next which makes life predictable and safe. The children of this world would create new songs nearly every day, and their complexity and beauty were nothing short of inspirational. Their harmonious voices seemed to be tuned to the drone of the wind chimes, and their voices would carry on the wind across the fjord and out to the sea. During these evening hours, it seemed the sea would dampen the roar of its 10 meter waves as though it too was listening to the sweet expressions of these beautiful beings.

Of course, hardly a night would go by without a song of history or exploration flowing forth from our voices as well. Singing for my queen and I was a spiritual experience. Our bodies would separate from our spirits inside that seemed to travel with the song. Our vocal abilities were facilitated by larynxes made for auto-harmony. The vocal muscles were formed of four ribbons, instead of the normal human voice box with only two vocal chords. Our voices were capable of producing pitches near the upper and lower ends of the spectrum simultaneously. With practice, they could also be controlled to produce harmonies while speaking or singing like two voices fed with the same lungs. There were sounds in our native language that cannot be made with the human voice. It is closer to Dolphin speech, or so my Earth friends tell me when I talk in my sleep. With two singers, a harmonious quartet was possible. When we sang epic songs, which we had learned from the most ancient trees, with poetic power, scarcely a child's eye would blink for up to ten minutes. The language was melodic anyway, but when put to music it was as though the creators of this tongue meant words to be sung rather than spoken.

I can easily recall the sounds in my mind, but this human body doesn't seem to be capable of making them. I still enjoy singing and still drift off into a song no matter how many times I sing it. Speaking is like singing for me. The cascading rhythm of voice and words with controlled pitch has turned speech into a sort of symphony for me. All humans can speak their various languages, but very few are actually masters of communication. It is not nearly so much what you say, but how you say it that conveys the most information.

The energy of the message is self-corrected by the energy of the being saying the words, and can be phase-shifted or Doppler-shifted by the energy of the being receiving the words. Tuning one's spirit to the frequency of love before venturing forth from the house in the morning, with attention on the reality that hardly anyone you meet that day will actually love themselves and will need your help to do so, will allow you to move through the population like a fish through forests of seaweed. It can be a little like driving fast on the freeway in moderate traffic. Gracefully, you can move from lane to lane passing cars driven by and populated with people who are unconscious. Once you get used to the awareness level, you can easily touch others as you pass by and watch them awaken. The love pulse you get in return is stunning. Like a straight shot of joy poured right into your heart.

When the evenings were over, and the children stood up from their seated positions on the warm speckled yellow stone floor of the terrace, there were plenty of hugs and smiles and sweet frequencies we could tell had changed them and us forever…again. As we walked them down the path to the cobblestone road one would always seemed to say, "We love Sariah." My queen would touch their soft brown hair and look deeply into their eyes with a love so pure and peacefully powerful no soul could imagine living without it. She could smile without parting her lips and seemed to direct her hair with the wind to frame that smile so that one's heart melted in her gaze and music seemed to play from every corner of one's body. Her skin would sparkle with tiny shards of colors as the energy from another being would flow over her like a solar wind. Her empathic abilities were the most developed of any being I ever saw on any planet. She often wore clothes to cover her entire skin including soft thin gloves to prevent her from being sensually bruised. But in the presence of the children her long and graceful neck and golden shoulders and arms were often bare without fear, for their thoughts and hearts were pure and caring. Her long arms and neck were so graceful and purposeful when she moved it was like sea flowers dancing with the ocean currents. "And so does the king," I would respond. To which they would chime as though part of a wonderful ritual, "Silly, you are the king," and they would giggle like birds running beside the road.

In the mornings, I loved to hike up the mountain that extended higher up the fjord above the house. With a small woven sack containing a few small brown rolls fastened to the sash around my tunic shirt, and a skin of water, I would move up the mountain path with large strides. This body was really quite amazing. It never tired, or had the burn of the muscles the way human bodies do. It could move perhaps 10 kilometers an hour at a walk and easily exceed 70 kilometers at a full run. Although it was a graceful and sensitive body, it was quite capable of war as well. I had the scars of ancient conflict.

39

Although I have been home many thousands of times, and have sensed flashes of battle, that is a door of memory I have never opened. To this day, even in this human body, I have a sense of motion and reaction that can only come from fighting in close combat. Sports always came easily to me, as I could track an object and predict its destination so as to allow the absolute minimum of energy to intercept its arrival. Several times I have, mere seconds before the event, known exactly where to stand to avoid being hit by flying shrapnel from an explosion or where to steer my vehicle to avoid even the slightest contact with a traffic accident occurring in front of me. I have learned and grown from those times and wish to remain the pacifist into which I have evolved.

The soil of the mountain was black, or nearly so, even when it was dry. It was living soil, full of microbes and nutrients that were perfectly balanced and able to perpetuate life forever. The entire mountain range was a single living consciousness, symbiotic in nature and fully aware of its purpose with the planet. To walk upon the soil with bare feet, or plunge the hands into its richness, would fill the senses with life force and a peace that comes from weathering all thinkings and doings of creation without changing course. The stone of the mountain was light gray and harder than most metals. Yet, with the proper sound, one could rend a piece from a slab or boulder like slicing cheese. Once the sound was ended, the stone would become hard again and useful for building or laying for roads. The sounds could be made with a few voices in harmony with practice.

From the ground grew trees of immense proportions. They stood over three hundred meters tall and some were as large a ten meters across. The bark was convoluted and rich with life. The skin appeared to be cracked open like the crust of bread than has split open from the force of the rising dough beneath it. It was a bright crimson red. And the cracks were deep and dark velvet red like old blood. The creviced bark was alive and emitted an ancient life force that would prickle my skin with energy. The trees on this mountain were more than one hundred thousand years old. They were the oldest beings on the planet and had memories ringing from them like great wooden songs of cataclysm and glory. I often heard winds and metal and the roar of flying machines and the crack of thunder from their souls. They were my teachers of the old times. It was part of the reason I liked hiking these mountains.

Like great red and bright green history books, they would whisper tales of abundance and scarcity that offered wisdom to beings with only a fraction their lifespan. I have returned from these mountains many hundreds of times, whether in this body or a human body, with melodies and aromas of melancholy joy like salty food mixed with sweet fruit in the mouth. Like returning from flight among the clouds, I would pace the inside of my heart waiting to refuel so I could get back up and soar like an acrobat tumbling through the clouds. The things I learned are woven through this book. They are as true as the laws of physics.

I once was considering with some colleagues the odds that a carbon-based universe would stabilize like this one, as opposed to any other type, such as one based on a different set of elements. I remembered what the trees and mountain taught me and offered it to the conversation. Like a memo delivered from an office across town

41

whose specialty it was to bake and sell pastries, it was so startlingly different than anything on the table that the meeting came to an end as though someone had turned off the fondue flame at the dinner table.

Leaving half-satisfied with their scientific conclusions, they were told that the universe we have is the only kind that could resonate with energy harmonizing at the golden ratio of Phi or 1.618 to one. The odds were no longer in question, as the possibilities were reduced to one. Hydrogen and Helium resonate at a certain frequency and will produce Carbon 12. Outside that frequency a small amount Carbon can barely exist. Silicon perhaps. But as it turns out, stars resonate at a certain, narrow frequencies depending upon their size.

Earth's Sun is a class "G" sun with spectra for Hydrogen, Potassium, and Calcium. Class "A" stars are the most common with Iron, Magnesium, and Silicon spectra, although they are still quite small as suns go in size. Class "O" stars are very hot and very luminous, being bluish in color; in fact, most of their output is in the ultraviolet range. These are the rarest of all main sequence stars. About 1 in 3,000,000 of the main sequence stars in the solar neighborhood is a Class "O" star. These giants have strong Oxygen, Carbon, Silicon, and Nitrogen spectra.

The race I recall from my meditations came from the third planet near the second sun in our system around two thousand years ago, in the time of Jesus, the region near Sirius was well known with a red glow. In modern times, that glow is not present. The red giant had indeed consumed all the planets in orbit around it, but had its corona dragged into a nearby black hole like water going down a bath

42

drain. Thus, the red glow was erased from the region, and all trace of the little system, once full of life and history, disappeared from sight.

Our people were sea-farers, musicians, and artists. We were philosophers and teachers. Our skills were greatly enhanced by being able to sense in the student the exact point of confusion, and by the ability to detach the spirit and see time forward and reverse like a headlight splashed down a dark highway. We were able to see the physical body move through time along fine paths of consciousness, connected to myriads of clusters of possibilities providing an almost infinite number of futures, all of which actually happen. The skill to develop is to sense the juxtapositions—those points in time when hundreds of paths connect in a single cluster—and to be able to detect the paths that resonate with the purpose of one's intention. Choices made at these junctures had immense impact upon the possibilities for futures. The trees and mountains have seen the entirety of intention on that world, and other worlds of entangled matter and energy, play out to the conclusion many times. That wisdom was added to the ability to see beyond time. In fact, time became an average of the consciousness of the universe with a very long sample line.

The coordination of our bodies and the speed with which we could move and think unfortunately made us perfect conscripts for the warrior race that became very interested in this planet. We proved uncontrollable and unbreakable by the methods of war and domination, and so were not widely utilized for actual fighting. Although we were not a patriotic people in the sense of going to war for anything, we valued our freedom above everything. When we were enslaved or conscripted, our minds would simply travel to the reaches of our imaginations. We were still free, just as you are each day you go to work at a job you hate. The wars of this world were short-lived and brutal. The planet's global cataclysms were like allergic reactions of the living planet-being itself vomiting violent races from her surface. It was as if the entire ecosystem could sense when the beings and the planet were not in harmony, which it corrected with quakes, tsunamis, or global storms to clean the slate. Our race survived because the planet told us where to be when the seas rose up and swallowed the great coastal cities, and when the great valleys were rent open like great furious sores gaping open to admit untold millions to the flowing lava inside the crust. The great trees of this planet preserved themselves over millennia by staying in the high mountains and connecting together into one planetary *being*. Through this giant nervous system they sensed the consciousness of the planet itself. The mountains were steep and unsuitable for high-density living, so the warlords left them alone. The trees had all the wisdom, and because we were able to sing the right tones and create the right symbols and icons, over time we were able to learn from them. We learned from the trees how to live in harmony with the planet. We learned how to position ourselves to survive. Our conscriptors didn't care about the songs, the legends, or the synchronicities with the planet. They only cared about stripping the minerals and fuels from the planet to feed their war machines. All their great technologies and fortresses and prowess ended as the planet expelled them from her and dashed their cities into sand with waves thousands of meters high.

The great valleys to this day are desolate and only grow prairie grass and small yellow flowers like a beautiful declaration that peace

44

and endless life will always succeed the intention of war. In the end, the planet won the war, and my race went home. Everyone that is except my queen and I. We chose to serve this world until it passed into the red sun's death.

Each month was cooler than the last. Although the sky was red and beautiful beyond belief, the plants took longer to grow, and the waters got colder, and the nights were becoming shorter. We lived each moment like it was the last we would be able to sing and dance and make love. The villagers were simple and full of joy with what they had. The two of us had traveled space. We knew of dying stars. One day soon this one would engulf this world and consume it.

I remember walking out on the yellow terrace one morning to watch the red Sun rise and listen to the wind chimes toning in the sea breeze, and the next thing I knew I was sitting beside a mountain stream as a nine-year old boy on the planet called Earth.

Le' olam,
Heaven folding,
Unfolding,
Enrapt in birthing;
Forgetfulness
Descending to the rich and green canvas
From which we pray.

Chapter 2: The Big Bang Never Happened

The arrow of time is a ray we measure in terms of distance. It is the human being who believes he alone occupies the zero point. We now know that the universe is the mathematical sum of the consciousness of all the sentient beings in it. Whether these beings are awake, asleep, conscious, unconscious, loving or fearful, they are affecting the average consciousness of the universe. Now, it can be said that the larger the population, the more stable the average value is. That may be the case with a population made of individual samples that never change in value. But sentient beings change all the time; sometimes through infinitesimal stimuli and sometimes through major ascension experiences. They oscillate. They vacillate. They are social beings who tend to coagulate into small groups around tribal campfires chanting similar ideas. When the range of ideas inside a group get too large, or when they become too dissimilar, then new groups form. Thus the average consciousness of the universe is shifting through the average of the averages, sometimes only a few units, and sometimes, especially after a major event, such as a revival or a mass awakening or a war.

The Big Bang is most widely accepted these days as the method by which the universe came into *being*. All the matter in the universe was packed into one *singularity* which is theorized to have formed through the collapse of everything in the universe into one spot. Sort of like a giant *inhale*, the universe drew all energy and matter into a single, one-dimensional dot.

Of course, conservation of momentum would demand that the large diameter universe, rotating at a very slow rate, would spin faster and faster as it collapsed like an ice skater drawing her arms in as she spins. This would mean that the universe would be spinning at its maximum speed possible, given its mass, which for all intents and purposes is finite. The *singularity* would be a possibility only. That is to say, locating the singularity and defining its speed would obey a Heisenberg uncertainty. This is a probability of its existence, rather than a pure center of the massive black hole universe. Spinning would change its shape, by way of the uncertainty, which would result in a universe that looks a little like a giant doughnut. The probability itself would create an opportunity for a Higgs event. Acting a little like Velcro, the uniformity of energy throughout the black hole would be highly improbable. Somewhere a snag occurred. Then, boom. Or rather, bang. The universe was born as the ice skater spun so fast that she exploded on global television, and within microseconds, energy was collapsing into the matter we see as stars and galaxies and planets.

This is the perspective of human scientists. Humanism is the basis for these assumptions. Picture a measuring cup in a sink under a dripping faucet. It would be easy to count the number of drops per minute, measure the water in the measuring cup, and then to predict the amount of time the cup has been sitting under the faucet. Right? After all, the conditions that were working to fill the cup were stable;

47

therefore, it is reasonable to make this judgment. That's humanism. The way things are, is the way they have always been, so we can extrapolate back to the beginning or to the future to make assumptions.

Wrong. You see, in reality someone placed the measuring cup in the sink, turned on the faucet for a few seconds, shut it off, and left it dripping just a few moments before you entered the kitchen. The cup has only been sitting there for less than a minute. This is catastrophism. Human consciousness is like the hand on the faucet making catastrophic changes to the universe.

But, according to modern science, Earth is once again the center of the universe. Or was that the church that made that claim? Oh well, I guess there's not much difference is there? I would like to propose a different analysis.

Consider the photon. When an electron associated with a shell of energy around an atom or a molecule falls from a higher energy state to a lower energy state, a photon of very specific frequency is emitted. This spectrum is so precise, that we can determine the exact identity of the atom or molecular bond—single, double, or triple and between which two atoms—by plotting it against time. Most stars generate spectra in the Oxygen, Carbon, or Nitrogen species.

However, when one looks into the night sky and considers for only a moment the distance between the star and the detector, in our case the human eye, an amazing realization comes forth. Arcturus is 36.7 light years from Earth and is nearly the same size as our Sun. This means that its light travels as fast as it can for nearly forty years to reach your eye at night. Well, that is from the human perspective.

48

From the perspective of the photon itself, it left the electron shell of its birth, and instantly arrived at your eye. There is no path forty light years long, weaving through gravitational fields and dodging particles throughout space, to get to your eye. Not from the perspective of the photon.

Impossible you say? Ah, but let us look at that math one more time.

Just a Little Math

$$e = mc^2$$

Really? Energy is equal to mass times the speed of light squared. What is the speed of light? $c = 300,000$ kilometers per second. Wait a minute. Let's express that while explaining all the terms.

$$e = m\left(\frac{300,000 \text{ kilometers}}{\text{second}}\right)^2$$

Now we can consider all the values in this famous equation. Remember we *are* the photon, and we are traveling at the speed of light. Time slows down as we approach the speed of light, which means that mass becomes very close to infinite. We physicists do not like the result of infinite.

Well, look at it another way. Time becomes zero, or at least very, very small. What did I say? Time becomes nearly zero. Put another way, everything in the entire universe—all the stars, planets, galaxies, clusters, and super-clusters—is located in the same spot. It's

49

all local. It's a *singularity*. It's all NOW. Since energy cannot be created nor destroyed, it appears that mass and energy have to pay the mathematical price. For instance:

$$\text{energy} = \text{mass x } 0.0000001$$ which means either energy must approach zero or mass must approach infinite as the speed of light is reached.

I am not, however, talking about *relativity* from inside the universe. I'm talking about relativity from outside the universe, which is where you are from anyway. In case the impact of this realization didn't sink in the first time, this is exactly what we would see from outside our own universe. The Hamiltonian of the universe is the potential energy plus the kinetic energy which equals zero.[2] You don't have to do the math. We're talking about looking at the universe, from outside the universe. That means we hypothetically step outside *relativity*, where everything in the universe can be explained in terms of other things inside the universe. Time is really distance at the speed of light, and we just proved that distance equals zero for the photon.

Since the set of energy in the universe is fixed, there cannot be an infinite resolution. If we can consider the universe from outside the universe, which mathematicians do all the time, and we just did right there, then we can observe the entire thing at once. Everything in the universe is NOW. Even if there was a *now* in the universe relative to everything else, we would not be able to calculate how fast it was going.

---

[2] The Hamiltonian is the sum of the Kinetic and Potential Energy of a closed system expressed in terms of momentum, position, and time.

Merely running the thought experiment of being the photon gives us access to all distance, which is all time, which is all local. This is consistent with the ancient Scriptures as well. God is omnipresent, seeing past, present and future all at once. It seems the only challenge here is speeding yourself up to match the speed of the photon.

Ah ha! We can do that. Empirically, we have seen thought move many times the speed of light, so speeding our consciousness up to the speed of light should be no more difficult than jogging around the park. That's easy for an awakened being. It is quickly being confirmed by the physics community that consciousness is integrally involved in the creation the universe. Isn't the sentience of humans and other beings driving the very observations that create the universe? Every single sentient being has its own reality. Currently, on the Earth, there are about seven billion sentient beings, each with its own reality. Each reality is unique.

The universe is the mathematical average of all these realities. If you have a country full of three hundred million people, the true reality of that country would be the average desire of every person in that country. Even communities and households are this way. If you boot out the bad people, the whole place becomes a nicer place to live. If you allow the bad people to gain leadership, the whole thing ends up in a handbasket.

The average consciousness of the universe is the collective reality most of us perceive, multiplied by our own reality. Two people can live in a small town. One thinks he is in hell. The other thinks he is in heaven. They are both right, once they multiply the presence of the town by their own reality. The population of Earth is so large, that the average reality is going to be statistically very stable. It isn't going to shift in value very much unless conditions independent of the individuals in the population change.

For instance, adding the Internet to the population allows people to meet, talk, love, and even solve problems. This one condition also provides unlimited knowledge to anyone who wants it. Knowledge empowers the individual, but when it is given to at least a critical amount of the population, the average awareness changes significantly. In fact, a population can actually evolve with this kind of empowerment. Religions, governments, creeds, and prejudices will change. The set of beings on the planet will change.

If you add all the potential energy of the universe to the kinetic energy of the universe, the result is zero. The result is NOW. The result is a singularity. This means that the Big Bang never happened. The universe is still a singularity. Time has been created by sentient beings like humans to allow it to exist as space.

Put more simply, you are the creators. You are sentient and are currently human in mortal form, or immortal form for some of you. You never die, you know. Your DNA is resonating with the energy of your environment. The environment in which the genes of the human body exists includes the consciousness of the being, the beings around the being, and the planet upon which it lives. The matter that makes up your body came from the planet. This one physical fact may entangle you with every other being on this planet, in fact with every element in the vicinity of the last super-nova in this neighborhood. This is the creation event that was engineered by the beings who live in this universe; namely, you. You did it.

The universe only exists because YOU are in it. If you leave, the entire universe would collapse as we know it. It is the power of your consciousness that allows it to exist in space and time. Neither of these two aspects even exists at the speed of light. The question is, "Why did you do it? Why did you slow down time so that the universe could exist?"

The reason is so simple. You did it so that you could drop out of the void of singularity to behold the love of one another. You did it to savor the taste of chocolate. You did it so that you could listen to music, watch children play, and wind blowing across the fields. You did it to watch snow falling and feel the rain on your face. Knowing everything at once is not heaven. The experience of life, struggle, being in love, creating life in one's own image, and even dying a mortal death is the purpose of your existence. And you exist millions of times. There is no such thing as existed, or yet to exist. This is only a perspective of yours. It all exists. It all happens. All of it. It is all possible. It is a potential of all potentialities. And the potential of it is only dependent on your ability to manifest its existence. That ability is empowered to the extent that you can remember the future and your past, which is the present. You are the only variable in the equation that you can control. So, do it on purpose and by all means, remember who you are, or were. Your birth here caused you to have a few years where your brain could not recall those experiences from your mortal lives you have accumulated. The brain is a lens for the human consciousness. By the time the lens gets clear enough to focus your consciousness from all times into this dimension, you have forgotten how to hold it. That is what I am going to do. I am going to train you how to hold the lens and focus it again.

Echoes,
Ripples across the face of the deep;
Pebble-lives dropped;
Forgotten dimensional interfaces
Between her lips and mine.

Chapter 3: Past Life

We can read that, "In Earth as it is in heaven," is also written, "as in heaven, so in earth," in the New Testament of the King James Bible.[3] Either way, it seems like it requires a little more practice for mankind to manifest the will of God in this Earth; keep in mind I may be talking about the human body or the planet Earth itself, as both are made of earth.

The moments during which the consciousness is extended like a crystalline fractal of our *third sight* into the void around us can be the most beautiful and also the most disorienting of our experiences.   In fact, third-dimensional existence itself, often called *real life* by most humans, can occupy the entire CPU of human consciousness when left to its own unconscious programming.   After all, we are either acted upon by the universe, or we act upon it.

We often look into the future or the past as we test one scenario or another in the crucible of our imagination. From a physics point of view, they are the same.   It is just as far from here to there, as it is from there to here. And time is actually measured in distance, especially in space.   In the singularity of creation, distance was zero because gravity was beyond escape; all crammed into that little space. In space, light-distance is the method by which we measure our

---

[3] King James Bible: Matthew 6:10 and Luke 11:2

universe at the light of speed. And at light speed, time becomes zero for the traveler.

Thought, as empirical data is now proving out, is immeasurably faster than light. We humans are evidence that thought is fast enough to escape the pull of gravity inside the singularity. Perhaps, it is not affected by gravity at all. What do you think that does to time in the universe? One's mastery of focus might allow omniscience to at least make momentary appearances, enough to provide testimony that such a circumstance really does exist. Time slows to zero at the speed of light, thus the entire universe becomes visible to us; past present and future. Mathematically speaking, all possibilities happen. Although it is difficult to process, our past is rather more difficult to expand to the potential of all potentialities than a past that does not involve us directly.

For instance, reliving a car crash, and accepting the reality of a different outcome that we experienced is not possible in this dimension. However, accepting *how* that crash affected us personally is possible. In fact, it can be vital to allowing us to learn what we designed to learn and to move on to a more merciful and clear position in the universe. The echoes from such a failure mode can preclude progress in the human psyche if it is not cleared like a hurdle on a running track. One will never finish the race in a single lifetime if we are standing in front of the hurdle in the middle of the track.

Divide by zero, or even a number very close to it, and we get infinite. Neither of these outcomes is desirable when seeking solutions that match our 3-D way of thinking, but let's face it. The universes are not really explainable in three-dimensional terms. They are balloons holding the energy of gods within them, collapsing into particles when mortality is desired and necessary, and existing as waves when unobserved. In fact, the distance waves travel is only relative to us, the sentients of the universe. For as we have learned already, it is our desire out of *source* for experience and existence that has sped time back up to create distance in the first place.

When distance numbers become too cumbersome, we utilize lunar distances, solar distances, and even parsecs to explain time. As it turns out, it is only the human consciousness that can truly consider this. The distance across a single atomic bond or the infinitesimal perturbation of distant suns by their unseen satellites are as easily contemplated as the assembly of a child's toy. We don't actually have a way to prove this, but it is widely believed that only human beings are capable of these imaginations. The Dogon Indians know from their earliest traditions that Earth is the 6th planet, not the 3rd. That is because they count from the outer planets toward the Sun. That is really quite amazing to hear, because Pluto was not discovered until the 19th century. The Dogons say that they are the people from the stars, although the permittivity of their existence belies this claim. That does not negate the pre-historic tradition that they are exactly correct in their perception of the motion of the galaxy and the origin of planets. Either they were taught by off-worlders about the universe far away from Earth, or they are surviving remnants of ancient travelers from other worlds.

You can't get there by car, or even by walking. These epiphanies can, however, be reached through meditation. It is how gods contemplate the smallest quanta and the birth of planets. It is how all creation occurs. It facilitates the blending of the conscious mind with the subconscious. The conscious mind, normally used to move the body about, or to satisfy one appetite or another, is completely different than the subconscious mind. We're not talking about the *unconscious* mind. This is another matter altogether, that will be discussed later.

One can easily find beings on all worlds who are unconscious, or who are simply not conscious that they are conscious. They are the ones who pass you on the sidewalk and emit no signal when they pass you by. One person to a car, they commute beside you oblivious to the world outside their rolled-up windows. They barely blink. They miraculously dress themselves each day and may even hold a job and give birth to children as a biological result of primal urges to act as though they are procreating the species, but they do not know who they are or where they came from. They scold their children for not being adults, and curse their own bodies for not allowing them to ever consume while maintaining the butt of a 16-year-old. They breathe air and drink all manner of concoctions and eat food, but they are not really alive. They are a vast sea of sleep walkers. They are like pylons in the parking lot through which the awakened humans weave for sport.

The synchronizing or tuning of the conscious mind with the subconscious mind is not easily done. Sometimes it can only be done for a few seconds at a time. Or, it can be felt like a shape in the fog during that layer between sleep and wakefulness. It is a difficult interface in which to dwell for any length of time, without practice.

The conscious mind considers and processes variables of inputs to the human being, while the subconscious mind is the actual operating system or the program that is running at multiples of light speed underneath the keyboard. Numbers, words, sounds, or other pieces of analog or discrete information are poured into the machine, and the subconscious mind cranks out the answers. Cells protect themselves against toxins, respirate, and even function quite well all the way up to the day they die without deviating from the program written at their birth. How does the program get written? What are the capabilities of the program? What inputs can it process? Are everyone's programs the same? Now you're thinking.

The program is stored in the liquid crystal of the cell walls of each cell in the community called the human body.[4] It's just a molecular layer of molecular switches not unlike a silicon chip, only made with carbon-based amino acids and proteins instead of combination of silicon and boron. That is simple enough. The binary code we have primitively utilized in our computers works on the same principle as the cellular processors, except that biological cells are able to process trinary, tertiary, and perhaps even more states of awareness. Zeroes and ones switching back and forth sounds like it would be fast enough, but it still takes three minutes to boot up a computer no matter what the clock speed might be. Cells, however, facilitate immensely complex algorithms that would humble the best game designer.

---

[4] This is a concept neatly discussed in *The Biology of Belief* by Dr. Bruce Lipton with his research of nucleus removal as part of the human genome project.

Consider the professional baseball player. Some observers would say that they are not the sharpest knives in the drawer. Closer analysis would prove otherwise. A baseball pitched at 95 miles an hour from the mound to the catcher's glove covers the distance in 0.463 seconds. The average human body takes 0.75 seconds to begin moving after a visual or audible stimulus. The complexity of seeing the ball released, tracking the ball with the eyes to the strike zone, moving the hips, legs, shoulders, and arms to hit the ball at the optimum millisecond in less than 0.463 seconds is not biologically possible. Yet it has been accomplished consistently by thousands of professional baseball players for more than 100 years. Observe a high-speed photo at home plate of the batter's face at the precise moment the ball is hit, and you will see his eyes, as though he was waiting for hours, looking right at the ball resting upon his bat. Equally amazing is the fielder who sees the ball come off the bat, begins sprinting to an instantly calculated point of intercept, tracks the speed and trajectory of the ball, waits until the exact moment, and dives forward at twenty-five miles an hour to catch the ball while he is weightless. Perhaps the baseball player is able to bring the subconscious mind to the moment of impact, operating hundreds of time faster than the conscious mind.

The cellular subconscious program never reboots, and it never shuts down, and it cannot be overwritten until the cell dies and is replaced through division of a live cell to replace it. By the time you are 14 years of age, every living cell in your body, except your brain, has been replaced.

Each cell functions on its own, usually in a manner that benefits the whole body, with or without a nucleus. Without a nucleus, the only thing a cell cannot do is replicate. Cilia move debris like the hands of a crowd might move a beach ball around an arena during a rock concert. Various liquids are produced to lubricate, dissolve, and even clean portals between the inside and outside of the body. Some cells face the outside interface and die by the millions each day like the soles of the feet, or the tips of the fingers. The program runs faster than any computer ever designed, and many hundreds of thousands of times faster than the conscious mind. Computers that match the speed of the conscious mind were invented in 2013.   That much is understood, but how does the program get written and what information is used to write it?

Simply put, it is the environment that influences the writing of the program. The temperature, humidity, toxicity, abundance, scarcity, and even the consciousness of the being itself and its surroundings are the bits of data used to write the program. Once it is written, it cannot be overwritten. That is to say, as long as that cell is alive, it will make decisions, respirate, protect itself from toxins, feed itself, and expel waste all automatically according to the last instruction. It does not need the nucleus, or DNA, and certainly does not need our conscious mind to carry out its functions. So again, how does the program get written?

While the cell is alive, the program runs. When that cell dies, a cell beside it replicates to fill in the missing spot. It knows to be a muscle cell, or a bone cell, or that of a nerve by a very mysterious process of differentiation, but the whole organism goes on living because of this process. The environment at the time of this division is what writes the new program. That is extremely important to consider, although we are not really advocating deathbed confessions here. All of the information accessible by the cell at the time of creation is utilized to write the subroutine by which this cell will operate is written unalterably at this time. As long as that new cell runs, it will run this updated program.

Now, you might ask yourself, "How does the new incoming cell know to become a muscle or a tendon, eye tissue or skin?" You may have been taught that it simply consorts with the cell next to it to get that answer. Well, then that stimulates two more questions. What if the cell needing replacement is at the exact interface between two radically different cell types? What if there are only two cells, such as a sperm and an egg? How do they know which cell is which?

Doctor Bruce Lipton, author of *The Biology of Belief,* told me personally of an electromagnetic image of the creature that serves as the extra-dimensional pattern by which the physical cells simply fulfill like a paint-by-numbers model. If you don't believe me, then attend medical school and find out for yourself. It's true. But think about it. Who makes the image of the being that the cells host? You do. That's correct. Your consciousness shapes and molds the very body that you occupy as a conscious being. The way you smile, exercise, comb your hair, lift things, and even feed yourself determines the shape of the vessel. You are the creator. You are the healer. And, you are the judge of yourself by your own state of energy that is completely under your control. Not even God can overwrite your self-judgment. It is a program rule that forms the foundation of the universe and without which the entire universe would collapse back to the singularity it would be without us.

So, let's consider the environmental factors. The energy level of the cell is like the charge on a battery. It is a few electron volts direct current. This DC level drops ever so slightly once the organism matures. Then a switch gets thrown that changes the way the power level is maintained in incoming cells. Somewhere around the age of 16 or 18, the cells begin to show age. They lose elasticity. They don't recover from injury as easily. The amount of sun damage, lack of moisture, overheating, overcooling, and level of nutrition for a cell changes its power level. Hormones flood the body, alerting it to the ever-pressing need to procreate, allowing it to change shape and function and prepare itself for falling in love. The cell resilience is switched to a subroutine, until it gets instructions from you. When it divides, the new power level is inherited by the new cell. Every 7 years, the organism has replaced every single cell in the body, except the teeth and the brain. These are not renewed once they are fully developed, at least under normal physiological conditions. No one has grown new brain cells after a stroke or regrown a tooth that has been pulled, or had a spot of decay heal itself.

For the rest of the cells, the total environment is considered. That means that if you are bathing your organism in hatred or fear, then the frequency and power level of either of those energies will be written into the new cell's program. If you are bathing your organism in self-love, the same holds true. The more time you spend in the frequency of love, the better the chances that the cells of your biological transducer, the body, will be replaced with the higher frequency written into your cellular program. In other words, the subconscious program of your body, which has always been an integral part of the soul, runs with a program that has been shifted to a higher frequency.

There are instruments and tools that can help the human being energize their own cells with new programming. The Lifestream Generator[tm] produces rotating DC magnetic fields pulsing at 7.8 cycles per second that bathe the cells in energy, producing a euphoric calm that can last for 24 hours after only a short exposure.[5] This magnetic field seems to recharge the cell's *battery*, so that if should happen to divide during this period of time, the new cell(s) are born with this new level of energy. This very effectively slows and reverses the aging process and has consistently shown higher cognitive abilities in test subjects. Holding these rods, simply sitting in the magnetic field for a period of time, will allow the cells to access this energy during the programming process of new cells.

This new level is free of fear and able to radiate a collective energy level that can actually be felt by other beings, which may be either in and or of their body. Those entities and sentient beings that can only be present in environments with higher frequencies will begin to make their appearance. Likewise, the entities and beings that are allergic to the light, like shadows chased by the sun, will not be present. The environment created by a human being can affect a sphere of unimaginable size. Without reservation, the awareness of this ability triggers a phenomenon called *awakening* or *remembering*.

This experience is called ascension. You will go through many ascension experiences, although you may have gone through many

---

[5] The Lifestream Generator is a product of Zero Point Research
www.zeropointresearch.com

lifetimes without one, and you may experience more than one in a single lifetime. Ascension almost always accompanies a realization that the spirit inside the biological transducer is eternal and has not only existed for eons of time, but has experiences, memories, and scripts that can be remembered into the current lifetime.

Let's talk about those right now. Experience is what it is. We gain it whether we are awake or asleep, alive or dead, aware or oblivious. Human experiencing Near Death often return to the living with a plethora of knowledge, sometimes altering their style of living because of it. The reality of the experience is entirely up for grabs. Like the optimist who believes we live in the best of all possible worlds, and the pessimist who fears that's true, it is the observation and interpretation of the individual that makes the reality. Where one person will love a film, the other will hate it. Where one person basks in the beauty of a piece of music, another person might be unable to resist the desire to turn it off. Where one person may love his job at desk number 101 on the 15th floor, the person at desk 102 may hate his job and can't wait each day to return to their reality. Where the person on one side of a kiss may melt into bliss, the other is looking at a watch.

To make matters even more complex and wonderful, experiences can be revisited an infinite number of times and yield even greater lessons and perspectives. And, each time they are visited – we call this *observation* – we recover a little something more. Like reading the scriptures, the level of love and inspiration will change each and every time the words are digested. During the decades I taught advanced Gospel Studies, I revealed to my students that the spirit with which the words were written are vital to consider when reading those words to get the maximum potential benefit from them.

The definition of a sentient being is one who can consider any experience and change his or her pattern or script based on the consideration of that information. Does this mean that a dog that cowers when you go to pet it, even though it has never been beaten in its entire life, remembers a wrathful master from its own past lives, and thus fits the definition of a sentient being? Yes it does, to a certain extent. Does it mean that a fish, instantaneously flitting from one path to another with a school of other fish is a sentient being? No. Instinct is not intelligence. On some level, a group consciousness is expressed, but sentience is not a quality shared by fish. By the same token, Dolphins and Whales are sentient beings who have joy, fear, and passion. They have been observed making love for pure enjoyment, and meditating while toning to the sea floor.

So, how does this have anything to do with past lives? Good question. Are past lives the process of our own manifestation and choice, or are they an energetic result of judgment by which we evolve? Better question. It is probably most important that we resolve this issue now, so that the perspective of spiritual evolution can be made more clearly to you.

Your spirit is eternal, existing as long as *source* itself. You are it, and it is you. You are not separate from it, but are connected to it in every way. It is the rational world of the third dimension that has been taught to you that masks this relationship. In a very real sense, you are god (small *g*). And, the world in which you live—that is to say the reality of the world in which you live—is your own design. The misery, joy, hardship, or bounty that you experience is of your own making. You experience mortality and the disembodied realms and gather that experience as matter of design, as haphazard as it might appear. This hit-or-miss kind of Pachinko[6] existence fits the pattern of chaos, rather than the harmony of construction as the energy follows the path of entropy. In order to avoid entropy, the lawful decay of energy due to random losses, one has to apply intelligence and intention. The point is that god decays into perfect chaotic entropy, when no intention is applied. When intention is applied things begin to build in a very real sense.

Now, your mind is about to expand, so relax a little bit. It won't hurt, but the room may spin slightly. Here we go. Whenever two energies meet in the universe, one energy will be greater than the other. When they combine, they will either constructively or destructively interfere with one another depending upon their frequency and whether they are in phase or not. This is better explained in the Chapter *Waking up in the Human Race,* but it pertains to past lives here, so listen closely. You are a single energy. You have a single spirit address. Polarized with you, like the other side of a single coin, is your soul mate. This is the single being that was made at the same time you took the square root of yourself to make two of you. When this being is added back to you, and this can be very temporary as the two of you meet from time to time in various existences, the

---

[6] Pachinko is a game whereby the player launches hundreds of small steel pin balls up into a vertical maize of pins. The balls then fall by chance through to either the game's storage box or into the player's tray, thus extending the playing experience. There are no other paddles to guide the balls like in American pin ball games.

energy level is so powerful that whole solar systems can be created. When the two of you enter a room, or a city for that matter, the energy will change simply with your presence.

The quality of the change depends upon you. You can bring darkness or light. The choice is yours. When you bring darkness, the frequency lacks light. That is to say you destructively interfere with the light that is there, consuming or cancelling out energy from everyone and everything. This is why tyrants tax their people and gain strength from the peoples' fears. They cannot actually produce anything, so they have other people produce while they consume. The really dangerous ones consume a thousand fold what they could actually utilize personally—such as food, sex, or entertainments—so that they can support the legions of protectors and their armies that produce nothing as well. The judgment is instantaneous and exact. The frequency of that energy will send vibrations out into the room, the city, and in fact the universe. Everything that can resonate with that vibration will begin sympathetically vibrating as a result of the exposure to that energy. Good cannot be accomplished with dark vibrations. It is a self-correcting system. This is how you judge yourself and why it is impossible for anyone to judge anyone else. Judge not that ye be not judged, lest ye be judged with that same judgment. Let me give you an example.

If you lean an acoustic guitar against its stand with the body of the guitar facing outward, and then turn up the stereo in your home, you will eventually hear a string on that guitar ring put like it was picked. In actuality, the guitar strong absorbed a certain amount of energy from the room at that exact frequency, because it sympathetically resonated with that frequency. If it could be measured, it would be called *absorbance* when the guitar string rang out like that. Everything in the universe has a resonant frequency, and thus absorbs energy from all kinds of sources, good or evil…light or lack of light.

In recent history, Asian governments wanted to develop a super-weapon in the form of viral agents. This required assembling a team of scientists, financing their efforts, and asking them to create this new weaponized illness. They gathered the most talented minds they could find and began the secret planning meetings. The design of death was among the darkest of energies ever assembled on the Earth. That conscious energy permeated the room and the building, although no one suspected their genocidal machinations. Their intentions were strong, and their design was shaping a defined focus. They were sequestered and supplied with meals so they would not have to leave for food or water. They were drinking bottled water. The security was so tight that every morsel of food and water they consumed was checked and rechecked.

According to the film *Water: The Great Mystery*[7], featuring the works of Masaru Emoto, their intention changed the arrangement of water molecules in the bottled water. Within hours, the entire team was rushed to the hospital deathly ill. No poison was found. Anywhere. Yet they had so energetically changed the water with the darkness of their intentions, that the water rearranged itself to nearly kill their mortal bodies. No antidote could be found, because it was the energy of the water itself that they had constructed with their own

---

[7] Officially Selected 2008 film by Gaia and Maui Film Festivals, Produced by Saida Multimedia www.waterthemovie.com

dark consciousness that poisoned them. As it turns out, Emoto effectively claims that water has a molecular memory. Now, the molecule itself does not change, but the unique way in which the water moves, in Brownian Motion perhaps, is affected by the consciousness of sentient beings who interact with it. Brownian Motion is the subtle juggling of molecules in liquid or gaseous states due to the movement of electrons in clouds around the molecule. The free electron pair on the Oxygen atom normally attracts the Hydrogen of another water molecule, but apparently the complex can be fatal as well as healthful.

The human body is made mostly of, and relies upon the quality of, water. When the water is structurally changed and osmotically flows through the cells, the activity of those cells is affected. Every spoonful of water we drink changes the chemistry of the body. In this case, the water did not promote health in those cells, but rather caused them to cease functioning correctly. The system of the universe may be self-correcting when it comes to resonating or supporting dark designs. The judgment is immediate and exact. That is so say, one cannot access a portal of light, or use the magic of blessings, if one is dwelling in darkness or practicing evil on someone.

These are laws of physics and mathematics. When you add the number 65 to the number 43, you get 108 every time in every dimension. When two or more frequencies are added together, the mathematic sum results instantly and exactly. The real lesson here is that the net frequency of the individual being is the result of the consciousness of that being. The real you inside that body of yours is more powerful that you can imagine. You are capable of incredible acts of creation, and as were destruction as well. The means by which you are able to do these acts is self-aligning according to the frequency of the being.

It is not like an IP address. That is to say, you are not the same frequency all the time. You are infinitely variable. Higher and lower, your consciousness shifts and flows like the wind moment by moment. It shifts while you are mortal very quickly, relative to the universe. It shifts very slowly when you are not in a mortal state, relative to the universe, because time slows down to nearly nothing. Everything in the universe becomes local to the wave-oriented person.

No, it's not metaphysics. It's physics. A photon in wave state travels at the speed of light, so it arrives at Earth the same time it left the star 8 light years away. Time is zero relative to the photon, while the speed of light is constant. The photon takes 8 years to each your eye, relative only to you.

The purpose of mortality is to apply one's consciousness to raise the frequency of the spirit while it is in the body, thus bringing the body to the level of light. You become a light body. From lifetime to lifetime, the relationship between the spirit and the mortal body evolves, or for that matter de-evolves, based on the environment, which integrally includes the consciousness. If the being is conscious that it is conscious, and thus can apply eons of experience while in the body, then the being can evolve with purpose and progress.

It is through meditation that they find the door way to the soul. There is nothing wrong with prayer, except that if you are doing all the talking and not listening, you will not be able to discern what the universe is trying to tell you. This book will provide you those tools that are needed to open this door. When the door opens, you will find yourself in a new place. It might be a green meadow, or a cave. It might be under the sea, or slowly drifting through the clouds. But it will be the same place for a long time. Then, you will learn to launch from this new place into the realms of time and space. Multiple futures and multiple pasts will fill your memories and teach you skills you could not possibly accumulate on one lifetime here on Earth. You will love, and die, and feel everything from a hundred lifetimes while still the flesh of a single lifetime, if you do this correctly.

It is not only essential for your evolution to perform regular meditation, it is vital for the planet. As these times and places become known to you, the richness of those experiences will add to the wealth of mortality.

After leaving your launch point in meditation, the consciousness is able to move through time, space, and dimensions. Understanding what you are experiencing from the perspective of a human being is nearly impossible. This is a little difficult to explain, so please have patience while this unfolds in this chapter.

I guess the easiest place to start is to consider if Adam had a belly button or not. According to the book of *Genesis,* Adam was formed from the dust of the Earth and had the breath of life breathed into his nostrils by the spirit of God. A full grown man—with no belly button—stood up with the spirit of a fully conscious being inside of him able to converse and reason with the gods who formed the Earth and populated then garden of Eden in the flesh. Yes, that's right. *Eloheim* means gods, plural. Okay?

Now Adam was fine for a full day, if you want to believe that a day of creation is actually a 24-hour day—perhaps a thousand or ten-thousand years if you want to believe that. It doesn't matter; either way. After he named all the animals on the Earth, which may have taken more than an ordinary day, the gods decided that he needed a helpmeet. In other words, out of all the beings on the Earth at the time—and there were perhaps millions of lower Adam—there were none of them with whom the gods wanted Adam to breed. They wanted to raise the gene pool with a *kadmon Adam,* or higher Adam. This meant that a new female had to be built that was genetically compatible with Adam. Twenty years ago, I could not have said this, but most of you now know that the best way to do this is to clone a perfect mate is from the exact same genetic material, and switch the sex genes to change the physical being from male to female. If this knowledge is not known by your year, it soon will be for that is how it is done—not seldom confused by the natural process.

This process is quite different than building an adult creature with no belly button. This is done by taking an egg and injecting the engineered human DNA into it. Keep in mind that human eggs were plentiful on Earth for there were hundreds of thousands of humans on the Earth at the time Adam was in the garden of Eden. They were of a Lower Adam breed. Adam was fully capable of breeding with these lower humans, and Cain did exactly that when he was banished from the company of his family and took a wife in the land of Nod.

The new female engineered for Adam was deposited into the womb of another female for gestation. It is not known whether the being was a lower Adam being, or whether the being was offworld, but it is mostly likely the latter. She had to be born, raised to young womanhood, and trained off world, because there is no record of

73

Adam taking care of a baby in the records. She was named Eve when she was brought to Adam in the Garden of Eden, like a marriage arranged by the gods many years in advance. She was conditioned in innocence and was strikingly beautiful, so the likelihood that she was raised around primitives in the general population of lower Adam is extremely remote. She would most certainly have been abused in such an environment. Raised with the gods offworld and then brought as a young adult to Earth, she was introduced to Adam who accepted her immediately, named her, and innocently let her wander the garden unsupervised. I am leaving the rest of the story to your individual tradition, as it is not necessary for this book. The point is that neither intelligences forming those two higher Adam human beings originated on Earth. Neither did you. We want you to remember who you are, because the planet and all the beings resonating with planet Earth right now need your total capabilities in order to properly complete the metamorphosis.

At the writing of this book in the year 2015, there are close to 7.9 billion humans living on Earth. There would have been more than this, but for the cataclysms. That is exactly why I wrote this and have returned to your time to give it to you. As we venture forward into the next chapter, consider that time is equally valid in both directions. If anyone gives you grief about accessing the whole timeline, tell them you're studying theoretical physics.

Reaching
Ever reaching into nova spawn
Seeking knowing;
Moving forward,
Back to memory's home
Of Is.

Chapter 4: Waking up in the Human Race

It is grand and daunting to think that an entire human race must be awakened and enlightened. It is possible, though. When I looked back into time to select the optimum time to begin the Spirit Race[8], I chose 2010 because it was the point at which enough people had reached a level of ascension and were ready to lead the world to the next level.

In every age there are a few humans who can master everything. In ancient times they were Shamans. At the end of medieval times, they were called Renaissance men. In modern times we called these people X-Factor humans.

It was discovered that in the social structure of societies, it takes only a small percentage of people to adopt a concept before it explodes into global acceptance. If this fraction includes X-Factor humans, then only a very small number of people may be needed to turn the world away from the precipice of societal self-destruction. The universe can fully be affected by taking action early enough.

The *Source* of the universe exists in each of us. We have memories in our very souls that are older than creation itself. We have

---

[8] The term "Spirit Race," was created by Ken Payne in Tell City, Indiana.

other memories as well.

Genetic Memories

There are genetic memories. Information coded into a series of amino acids making up DNA is passed from one descendant to the next, perhaps over hundreds of generations. Not only are the propensities of the parents inherited by the offspring, non-congenital traits can be passed along as well. Talents are often shared with family lines. Just as the genetics of champion racehorses are highly valued for their proven ability to produce successful racehorses from the colts, human traits are passed down as well. The ability to sing, play baseball, act, or play musical instruments is passed from parents to children.

Although it was believed for millennia that we are only a product of our genetics, this has been disproven. The idea that the nucleus of a human cell is the brain of that cell has been completely refuted. The nucleus of cells can be removed, and yet the cell continues to respire, consume food, expel wastes, and even protect itself from toxins. The very same functions it performed when it had a nucleus. Only when the cell dies, and needs the genetic material stored in the nucleus to be able to duplicate itself, criticality of the absence of the nucleus realized. The life-cycle of the cell ends, never to procreate again.

There are numerous studies that show that people often have behavioral traits of their ancestors. Still an emerging science, the study of genetic memory is gaining many supporters. The idea that an ancestor could learn a skill or a personality trait that is somehow encoded onto the DNA, and then that DNA is passed to a descendant, is theoretical. For instance, healthy mice treated to develop diabetes will give birth to offspring that spontaneously develop diabetes. Additionally, the ability to play music, throw a ball, paint pictures, or even leadership traits passed down from one generation to the next are well documented, even in case studies where the child was adopted and did not have any exposure to the biological parents.

Light Memories

There are light memories. Light itself is just a form of energy. Each photon is a particle without mass that carries information. When left to travel through space unfettered, a photon displays properties of a wave. This wave will last forever relative to us here on Earth, unless it runs into something and is subsequently annihilated. This information is transferred to the target that is impacted by that photon. Normally, photons are sent in a beam of information that leaves the source in a random direction. The distance between the two electron shells is absolutely mated to the frequency of that photon. That is to say, Potassium that is volatilized in a flame will generate photons in the red color band, and Sodium will produce a yellow flame. Those photons can be detected by a solid-state device and qualitatively identified as Potassium or Sodium without any doubt. Bonds between atoms in a molecule, by stretching or bending caused by a specific wavelength laser probe, will also be revealed just as repeatably.

There are also patterns of photons that provide information. Our eyes are designed to respond to photons that strike specialized cells called rods and cones. Those inputs are deciphered by our brain and turned into images that very closely resemble our world. Photons outside of the sensitivity of those cells, or outside the experience of the brain, will not register to humans. For these photons we humans might need something else. We might need an instrument to detect these photons. We might need training to allow our brain to see something that is happening around us. There are most certainly energies in the form of waves or particles around us that are hitherto undetected by us. As soon as the particle's spin in observed, however, it immediately drops out of being a wave and displays properties of a particle.

Niels Bohr's Principle of Complementarity, in essence, states that there may be more than one accurate way to view natural phenomena. The idea that light displays characteristics of both a particle and a wave took physicists many years to agree upon. Bohr argued that even if observations may appear to be in conflict, both viewpoints are needed in order to form a more complete understanding of an object or event. As he once explained:

Fig. 4. Niels Bohr 1885–1962

"The opposite of a correct statement is a false statement. But, the opposite of a profound truth may well be another profound truth."

Bohr was a visionary in the field of quantum mechanics. His ideas of the structure of the atom are still standard instruction in chemistry and physics. After moving to Manchester, England to work with Ernst Rutherford, he became interested in the model of an atom whereby the electron was featured hovering around the nucleus. We used to say it orbited around the nucleus, but a better understanding was that electrons existed in a *probability shell* that was unique in distance from the nucleus depending upon the number of protons in the element(s). He made a refinement on the idea that the negatively charged electron did not fall into the much larger positively charged nucleus to emit light. In Bohr's model, he proved that electrons are actually excited into higher states or shells, and that it was actually the quantum leap – yes, this is a very *small* distance not to be equated with large leaps made in movies and pontificated by various folks who want to sound important – to the lower the energy state, or shell, that the light is emitted in the exact wavelength of that distance between the shells. Einstein called Bohr's theory, "The highest form of musicality in the sphere of thought." The interesting quandary was this; there was no way to predict when or in what direction the photon of light would emit. It shook the very foundations of science and, as it turned out, religion as well. The question, "Was there an objective reality that existed whether or not we could ever observe it?" could not be answered.[9]

Einstein once had a healthy argument with Ernst Mach about Newton's Bucket. Newton offered a hypothetical condition of a bucket hanging from the ceiling by a rope. The bucket was filled halfway with water, and then the rope was wound up by rotating the bucket by hand. When the rope had about one hundred turns on it, the bucket was released to unwind. The question was this: "What does the surface of the water appear to an observer inside the bucket?"

The answer is that the surface of the water will curve due to the centrifugal force of the spinning bucket, as the water catches up to the bucket that is spinning while the rope unwinds. Mach's argument is that Newton dismissed relative motion too readily, but then made an even more startling observation. The observer, as though in a small boat on the water in the bucket, actually sees a motionless bucket while the room revolves around the bucket. So Mach posed another

---

[9] *Einstein* by Walter Isaacson copyright © 2007 Simon and Schuster pg. 321-322

question: "How does the surface of the water appear if the bucket is stationary, and it is in fact the room that is spinning?" The answer is that the water would curve exactly the same way.

In 1918 Joseph Lense and Hans Thirring obtained approximate solutions of the equations of general relativity for rotating bodies. Their results show that a massive rotating body drags space-time round with it. This is now called 'frame dragging' or the 'Lense-Thirring effect'. In 1966 Dieter Brill and Jeffrey Cohen showed that frame dragging should occur in a hollow sphere. In 1985 further progress by H Pfister and K Braun showed that sufficient centrifugal forces would be induced at the centre of the hollow massive sphere to cause water to form a concave surface in a bucket which is not rotating with respect to the distant stars. Here at last was a form of the symmetry that Mach was seeking.

Frame dragging has recently been verified experimentally. This involved using the rotating earth as the massive body and putting a satellite into orbit with a gyroscope which kept it pointing in a fixed direction. Although the Earth has only a tiny frame dragging effect it was possible to detect the extremely small precession of the gyroscope which was caused.

You see, it is the *relative* difference between the bucket and the room that makers the water curve. In other words, if you were in a small ship on the surface of the water in the bucket, what you would see is that the water was curved and that it was the room that was spinning around you. Their proof implied that if the bucket was stationary, and it was the room that was spun around while the rope

81

pivoted on a swivel, the water would still curve! It is therefore a very solid assumption that our universe is curved based on the idea that it may be spinning *relative to another universe outside of our own.* Like a balloon around a balloon, the two universes have curving effects on each other. This is important to remember, as we compare our own souls to others around us.[10]

As I build the foundation for the proof that the Law of Attraction is actually a process that can function reliably and in a repeatable manner for ay human that learns how, please have a little patience as I enter a couple more experiments to make sure you don't have any doubts.

In 1799, Thomas Young initiated his medical practice in London. His primary interest was in studying sensory perception, and while still in medical school, he discovered how the lens of the human eye changes shape to focus on objects at different distances. While pursuing his interests in the function of the human eye, Young discovered the cause of astigmatism in 1801, which was about the time that he began his study of light.

[10] **November 2004 MacTutor History of Mathematics** [http://www-history.mcs.st-andrews.ac.uk/HistTopics/Newton_bucket.html]

Fig. 5. Thomas Young 1773–1829

In 1801, Young began a series of experiments with light pattern interference. He observed that when light from a single source is separated into two beams—like when a flashlight shines on a dark piece of paper with two slits cut into it—and the two beams are recombined onto a screen a few feet away, the combined beams produce a pattern of light and dark fringes. Young concluded that these fringes were the result of the beams of light behaving as waves with their peaks and troughs either constructively or destructively interfering with each other. When this occurred, alternating lines of light and dark resulted.

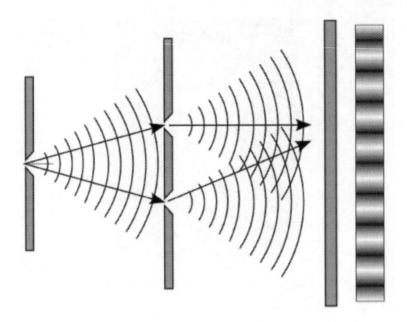

Fig. 6. Thomas Young's double slit experiment

What became apparent, in Young's conclusion, was that different light waves interacted with one another in and out of phase to either annihilate one another to darkness, or add to one another for greater brightness. When two energy signals come together, they either constructively interfere with each other, thus adding to the power making them brighter, or they destructively interfere with each other, causing a cancellation of the signals making them darker. The light and dark lines on the right side of Figure 7 show this very clearly.

The dark lines are a visual version of what noise-cancellation headphones do for eliminating room noise. The small microphones on the outside of the headphones pick up the room noise. The pre-amplifier inside the headphones makes an equal and opposite sound, and plays it along with the music you want to hear. The room noise is magically reduced to almost nothing, because the two opposite sounds cancel one another out.

Oh that we could have small microphones that pick up the tiny negative energies around us and collect them into a single signal. Then we could shift the phase of that negative energy and then overlay it upon our negative life energy. The result would cancel out any negative signals in our lives.

In the future, many people bringing their positive energies together have a mighty effect, even on the very structure of matter itself. Whether it is water, tissue cultures, or the health of a human being, the constructive interference of positive signal has a great effect for good. Likewise, collecting and echoing the negative energies in the world have the expected effect.

Our suggestion is that beginning from the year 2010 you turn the continuous television news programs off. Every hour, the news actors or ticker tapes feed negative stories to your living rooms, adding a resonance to your lives that is negative. Do not let their need for ratings and thus advertising dollars perpetuate and breed the negative energy that tears down all the good done in the world. Nikola Tesla proved through his resonance experiments that a small amount of energy added precisely to a metal beam rebounding from a previous input would cause that metal beam to fail eventually as if overloaded by a much larger weight. This constructive interference with a very small weight at the exact right moment made the metal beam look like it was being bounced upon by an eight-hundred-pound gorilla, when in actuality the weight was only five pounds.

85

The dark lines in Young's double slit experiment are not the source from which to draw happiness. The bright areas resulting in light added upon light are the most likely places for positive energy to be found.

Atomic Memories

There are also atomic memories laid into us at birth and added to as we consume matter for food, and as our cells are replaced with new matter from that food. That matter may contain particles that are entangled with sister particles possibly created by the same ancient super-nova.

These particles act like molecular transmitters of our intention across space and time. Sister particles may exist in other humans alive on the Earth now, souls embodied on distant worlds now or even as parts of other worlds now. The common thread is that these particles are entangled always in the *now*. There is no future or past to consider. Every effect, one way or the other, is exactly in the *now*. It is not that a future or a past does not exist. It is that these energies exist independent of time. They may be multi-dimensional in nature, so that they are not limited or slowed down by a requirement to satisfy three-dimensional physics as we know it.

All humans emit energy into the universe through their biological transducer; the human body. Most people do this in an unconscious manner. They think their thoughts, and act on those thoughts, unaware of the effect they have on the universe. Most of these people function out of fear. That is to say, the energy they generate is a result of their response to the environment around them. One person has an effect. One billion people in the same state of fear have an unimaginable effect on the entire universe.

Where did these entangled particles and energies come from? The theory that the universe came into being from a single big release of energy from super-compressed matter is fairly well accepted. The observation that humans can comprehend the smallest quantum energy and particle, as well as the birth of solar systems, lends power to the idea that we may have been, and yet still are, involved in creation itself.

Energy, raw and chaotic, tends to wind down like a clock in agreement with the 2nd Law of Thermodynamics. As energy moves away from its point of release, emanating in all directions at once like a sphere, we calculate that it decreases at the square of the distance traveled. The further away from the source the energy is measured, the lesser the concentration of that energy. It is sort of like money at the end of the month not being able to make all the bills that have come due.

If a firecracker exploded in the middle of a football field, persons standing at the forty-yard line would hear much more volume than those standing at the goal lines. Beside the sound expanding at the square of the distance, the very air molecules that allow the sound to travel to the listener also reduce that energy to the point that the sound pressure may be completely absorbed to inaudible levels. Three hundred yards away, that firecracker may be completely inaudible. The sound expanded out in all directions with a fixed original energy. As the volume of space increased, the amount of energy available to go into your ears was reduced by the square of the distance. This energy moves through space in little packets.

Each individual packet of energy, called quanta, can change state almost at will. Whose will? Great question. Hopefully, the answer will light a fire inside of you. What is meant by changing state? Energy can exist in one of two states that we will consider.

One state is called a wave, or a vibration. The other state is called a particle, like a proton, electron, or photon. There are even smaller particles, but in our spacetime they exist for perhaps a millionth of a second before disappearing. These states are important to understand, so here we go.

There is an event in the universe that occurs randomly that releases immeasurable amounts of high energy. It is called a super-nova. This is one of the stages in the death of stars of a minimum mass. We don't really know how large a collapsed star mass can be to form a super-nova, and we are surprised when they occur. We suspect that they have to be at least 1.4 times the size of our own sun in order to display this stellar death sequence. The consensus is that suns of sufficient size to go super-nova are perhaps hundreds of times denser than our Sun. We are also very happy all super-novas have occurred very far away from Earth, so far. When a star that mass or larger loses its explosive drive, gravity begins to tip the natural balance between blowing up and collapsing completely. Now, there are a couple of forces at work here, so here they are.

When an ice skater begins to spin, and then draws her arms in tightly against her body, the speed of her spin increases incredibly. She can spin so quickly the TV cameras can't capture the movement with anything better than a blur. This principle is called conservation of momentum. There is a certain amount of energy contained in her diameter and spin. If she decreases the diameter, then the rate of spin must increase to balance the equation. The same thing happens with shrinking suns.

As gravity compresses the size of the sun, now no longer exploding, its revolutions increase. For example, if our sun were to reach the point where it was collapsing, the revolutions would speed up from about twenty-eight days to hundreds of revolutions per second or more. Nevertheless, the same mass of this massive sun would occupy a smaller and smaller space as it collapses further and further. Then a moment occurs with that massive sun that is rare and remarkable.

The electrons that used to exist predictably in probability clouds around hydrogen protons, which are now helium nuclei, can no longer remain in their quantum probability clouds at a likely and safely reactive distance. The inter-molecular gravitational force becomes so great that the electron is pulled down onto the proton. The proton is neutralized by the electron, forming a neutron. At first, this occurs a few atoms at a time. As the collapse continues, more and more neutrons are formed. Sort of like rope that is stretched to its limit by a heavy weight, first a few fibers snap, then a few more. Finally, a point is reached when the remaining fibers can't hold the weight, so the rope

89

completely fails. During this chain reaction all the remaining electrons fall into protons in an instant.

This event creates a tremendous explosion called a super-nova. The remaining atmosphere of the star is sheared off, and the most powerful radiation imaginable shines out into space, converting entire solar systems into raw energy as it blasts into space. This energy is single in source, providing enough power to form higher elements well beyond the molecular weight of iron. If it were not for super-novas in the universe, eventually all matter would become cold and lifeless iron. This is apparently a creative event that replenishes the upper-order elements throughout the universe.

The important thing to remember here is that the energy it took to form these higher elements was singular in source and synchronized all the matter in its creative path. It is believed by most physicists in our day that super-nova events happen all over the universe.

It is also possible that medium *bangs,* as opposed to *big bangs,* resulting from the Higgs processes and causing black holes to explode occur on a fairly regular basis in the void at the outside of the universe. It is known at this time that these structures are mathematically extremely stable, and that thus it takes something anomalous to make the black hole explode into the void. A Higgs condition is a little like balling up Velcro. The little hooks get caught up in the little fibers, resulting in a sort of rubber-band backlash if they ever get a chance to come loose. This may be the little rip in the somewhat seamless fabric of a black hole. These energy events release enough energy to create whole galaxies, much of which contain these entangled particles and entangled energy. Hold that thought.

Entangled Particle Theory

There is a principle called the *theory of entanglement* that we mentioned in the beginning of this chapter. This term can involve energy or particles. For some reason, as yet still unexplained, pairs or groups of particles can demonstrate a remarkable property. We will discuss the experimental treatment of this later. Experimentally, two small particles can be "picked" off of a large particle using an electron capture detector and separated by incredible distances.

At first, the distances were a few millimeters. Then, in a stunning demonstration, they were separated by eleven kilometers. In the year 2015, beryllium ions are utilized like atomic switches in the BIM's for deep space communication. BIM's are Beryllium Ion Modems, capable of transmitting binary data instantaneously across any distance without any loss of power. The original Mars rovers, Spirit and Opportunity utilize the old fashioned radio style transmitters. It took hours to get simple data back and forth from Earth to the rovers. The latest generation of Mars robots utilizes BIM's for communication. It greatly reduces the power needed for transmission and uploaded instructions, as well as the bandwidth. The high-definition video coming back from these rovers allows far better efficiency with the mission. The folks at Cornell University were very happy when BIM's became available on deep-space programs.

Here is how it works, generally speaking. Each particle has a spin quality. Like a little planet, each one spins on its tiny axis. Some spin in a fashion we call plus one-half, and some spin in a fashion we call minus one-half. Typically, a given electron cloud on an element will have a nearly even number of each, obeying the Pauli Exclusion Principle. The spin of one particle can be changed by a technician through small, electromagnetic pulses. Instantaneously, the sister particle—called an entangled particle—changes spin as well. As it turns out, it is at least thirty times the speed of light…perhaps much faster.

Entangled particle theory has experimentally proven that particles change spin instantly, if the sister particle has its spin switched. The Alain Aspect thesis in the 1980's claimed that ions could "communicate" at a distance at speeds apparently many times the speed is light. It has been repeated many times and at distances exceeding eleven kilometers, which might as well be across the galaxy at the quantum level. Einstein called it, "Spooky action at a distance." Currently, there is an argument about whether the communication takes place between the two particles at all and whether they may actually be the *same* particle existing in two places at once. This is important, because the particles that make up the Earth also make up the human body.

The most incredible aspect of this repeatable process is that it does not matter how far these particles are separated. Instantaneously, these particles change spin identically. The reason is unknown. The effect is irrefutable.

The importance of this *switching* action is that it acts just like a binary code. One spin direction is zero (0), and the other spin direction is one (1). Plus one-half and minus one-half are good discrete values that can be used in binary code. This means that with a small bank of these ions, and a spin modulator, a modem can be designed. In the year 2015, we call them BIM's, named after the original Beryllium ions that were used to make the first deep-space modem.

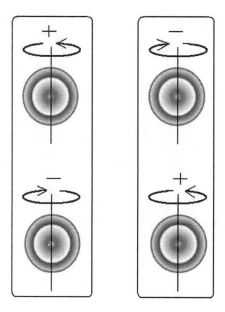

Fig. 7. Particles on the top row are flipped, and the sister particles change spin instantly, creating an atomic particle switch.

Now, back to the thought. Energies and particles can be entangled across a great expanse of space. What affects a particle in one area affects its sister particle the same, possibly even across parsecs of space and time, instantaneously and without any loss of power. This exchange of energy is an exchange of information. Yes, energy transfer is the same as the exchange of information. Like genetic code passed from parent to offspring, or electricity applied to one end of a copper wire from one telephone to another telephone, the movement of energy is the exchange of information.

There are some really fascinating things we discovered that you need to know. Humans are capable of generating magnetic fields. These fields are normally in a nice, symmetrical star tetrahedron around the human body. This three-dimensional geometry is shaped like this:

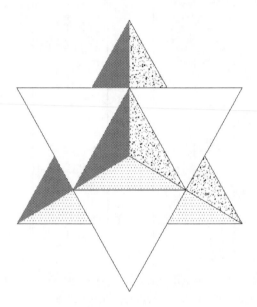

Fig. 8. The star tetrahedron

This form is the first stable geometry in the third dimensional universe. It is also the shape of the energy pattern of human consciousness. It is called the MerKaBa. **Mer** refers to a specific kind of light that was understood in Egypt during the 18th Dynasty following the reorientation of religions toward the worship of a one

God of all creation. "Mer" was seen as two counter-rotating fields of light spinning in the same space. These fields are generated when a person performs specific breathing patterns, which will be explained later in the book. **Ka** refers to the individual spirit of a person. **Ba** refers to the spirit's interpretation of its particular reality. In the human reality, Ba is usually defined as the body or physical reality. The three sounds together explain how the rotating fields of light, the spirit, and the body together function like a biological transducer to both sense and transmit to the universe.[11]

It is also the shape of the equatorial life energy pattern around the Earth. It forms the radial axis of a grid of energy that circumscribes the human body, and when it is energized through human intention, it connects human beings to the grid. Some of you may not be familiar with the *Christ Grid*. It is reported to be a fixed grid of energy lines that are linked to the planet at large mountains. This connection may be the connection to Source through which *downloads* of various inspirational content comes forth.

These MerKaBa fields can be programmed with the intent of the individual. If the human is angry, then the field may appear distorted and energetically chaotic when viewed with instrumentation capable of detecting these magnetic fields. If the person is sad, then it can be nearly motionless and the points of the tetrahedrons have been observed with instruments and through Kirlian photography to be misshapen and actually not symmetrical.

---

[11] Also taught by the Flower of Life Research Center and assembled by Drunvalo Melchizedek. www.floweroflife.org/tmerkaba.htm

In truth, the human geometrical magnetic field is a good reflector of the energy of the human being. Without getting into details beyond the scope of this book, we want you to know that these fields can be manipulated by the individual to great levels of power. They can also be left idle in ignorance. The effect on the particles and energies of the human is measurable and profound. The proteins of the human body come from the genes of the human cell. There are not enough human genes to account for the number of proteins in the human body. This means that the human gene is capable of making a large variety of proteins, the choice of which is greatly influenced by the environment. That environment is widely accepted now to include the human's consciousness.

You see, the three-dimensional body of a human being is made of cells, which in turn are made of molecules. The protons that make up those molecules are not all the same. The population of protons, for instance, has a range of weights.

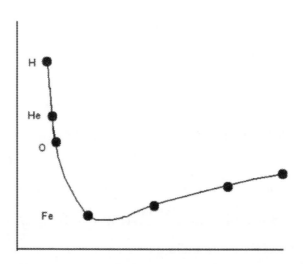

Fig 9. Protons are not all created equal. Hydrogen (H) is the heaviest, dropping to Iron (Fe) and then slowly gaining weight to the heavier elements.

Hydrogen is the heaviest proton, and Iron contains the lightest. Many physicists believe that the universe, through the irrefutable process of entropy, will eventually all decay to Iron. This is important to understand. The loss of this tiny amount of mass when Hydrogen fuses to become Helium, times the speed of light squared, is why nuclear explosions are so powerful. The question that continues to baffle physicists is, "What part of the Hydrogen proton was lost when two joined to become Helium?" We keep smashing the little beggars apart at CERN, and we can't figure out which part is emitted as energy when different elements are formed, or where the energy comes from to make the heavier protons.

Each cell is a living thing in need of its own nutrients and waste management. For a human body, this respiration process is done as a very complex system or physiology that is a cooperation between specialized cells benefitting from the function of every other cell in the body. Each cell needs a fresh supply of oxygen and fuel to maintain life and reproduce according to the genetic design and maintenance process. Those nutrients are formed of molecules, which are formed of atoms and subatomic particles. These very particles can be entangled with other particles and other energy in the environment of a planet or other planets forged by the same super-nova event.

Those molecules form minerals that exist in the soil. Those minerals are absorbed and utilized by plant life to make beans, leaves, fruits, vegetables, and so on. These plants are consumed by humans, cattle, fish, and birds. One way or another, the bones, muscles, and other tissues are constructed from the particles that are entangled with other particles on this world, and upon other worlds made during the same super-nova event.

So, when we say, "You are what you eat," we mean it. What's more, it means that over time we may accumulate a new set of extremely advanced and highly sensitive *sensors* in the body that pick up the energy fields generated near particles in other human and animal bodies, in this planet, or on other worlds. Some of these fields are not so much made by the physical body as they are by the energy body of other sentient beings. These energies are transferred into the energy of the particles and energies that are entangled, and then these particles and energies have instantaneous effects on other energies and particles throughout the universe, which may have been created simultaneously from the same super-nova event. So, when we say that everything you do will eventually affect the universe, that is exactly what is happening.

Now it also is very evident that everything we think about, or intend, also has an effect upon the universe as well.

Remember the guitar experiment we ran previously in the book? A certain frequency in the music *resonated* with that guitar string. In actuality, the string *absorbed* that exact frequency out of the music in the room. This sympathetic energy transfer is how each of us affects the universe. It is also how all information is moved through all dimensions regardless of time. It is how information and knowledge is moved to you as well.

This is a very important concept for you to understand. Life energy resonates with a human soul regardless of its source or whether it is positive or negative. The effect upon any individual soul by this Life energy depends completely upon the vibration of the soul. That vibration, or frequency, is only in the control of the soul himself. The frequency at which you will resonate is entirely your responsibility. The responsibility for the tuning belongs only to the individual. If you are tuned to a vibration that will not be affected by anger, then someone's anger toward you will not affect you. If you are tuned to a vibration that will not resonate with jealousy, then you will not feel or be affected by jealousy. If you are tuned to a vibration that is not love for yourself, then you cannot resonate with the love of anyone.

If you were to learn anything from this, we want you to learn to be more self-centered. Once you are centered more in yourself, specifically in your heart, then you will reach what I call the Janus point. This is the point at which you will see clearly the past and the future, but more importantly that although you exist in the *now*, your observation of the time arrow before you and after has a profound effect. After all, from a physics point of view, it is just as far from LA to San Francisco as it is from San Francisco to LA. Time is nothing more than distance at a rate of change.

Fig. 10. Janus is the dual-faced god of gates. Seeing the past and future of the time arrow empowers us to use the Observation Effect to the advantage of the universe.

We want you to become sensitive to how Life energy works. If you can feel it and learn how to unravel the scripts of past mistakes and misconceptions, then perhaps you can take full responsibility for that energy. And if you can take full responsibility for that energy, perhaps you can awaken to your full potential.

Our observation of any event, past or future, has an effect. We use advanced instruments to see things we cannot see with our eyes. Just because we cannot see things with the naked eye, does not mean they aren't there. For instance, pollen affects the mucous membranes of some people. People had a hard time believing in such things, until one was photographed using an electron microscope.

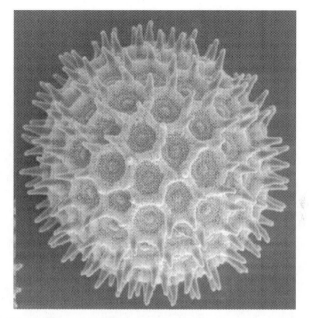

Fig. 11. Pollen at 20µm magnification. Image courtesy of WikiCommons).

One might think this is an accurate rendition of the pollen spore. Not true. The pollen was altered by its bombardment by electrons to produce the image. When we shine a light on something to see it, because we need the light photons to strike our rods and cones in our eyes in order to see something, that subject is actually, although infinitesimally, being affected by those photons. Thus, our observation of that subject changes that subject.

When we look at a past event, the impact of that event changes from our perspective. That does not mean you can affect anything or anyone else in your past, but you can change how it affected you. That's exactly the objective of self help.

For example, two people are taking lunch as a small table at an outside café. While they are quietly involved with each other, there suddenly occurs a traffic accident in the street right next to them.

Of course, the police were called and the drivers were interviewed by an officer. He then noticed the couple sitting at the roadside table. Approaching them, he asked if they had seen the accident. He pulled out two new sheets. How many versions of the accident does he have when he finishes? You guessed it. Four. The two drivers and the two diners all gave different recollections.

About this time, the restaurant owner comes out and says that he has a video surveillance camera that has a clear view of the street. The six people then went back to the manager's office to view the tape. Within a few minutes, everyone knows exactly what happened. The four police reports are brought into a state of full corroboration.

Observing the past with a clear vision clears the distortions away and allows the full energy of truth to flow forward. The same thing happens when we review past events in our own lives.

We want to begin the process much earlier, so the human race can walk freely away from the path inherited in the year 2015. If the greatest teachers of Earth taught us anything, it was embodied in the two great commandments of Christ:

> "Thou shalt love the Lord thy God with all thy heart, mind, and strength, and the second is like unto it. Thou shalt love thy neighbor as thyself. Upon these hang all the laws and the prophets." Matthew 22:37–39

I would like you to also pay attention to the fact that this was originally written in Greek. Greek logic usually states the conclusion first and then the premises to that conclusion. In other words, if we were to read this in the order in which it was said, and not written, it should read:

> " Love yourself, and then you will be able to love your neighbor. By doing this, you are loving the Lord your God with all your heart, mind, and strength."

It is easy to see that Christ was teaching people to love themselves. Without this love, nothing is possible but despair and darkness, which are also great effects on the universe. Hopefully, these are not the effects you want to have on the universe. We are about to unlock the secret for you, so you can have the effect of light. Keep in mind that fear is far more powerful than love. A woman came to a priest friend of the authors to ask for help. She had contracted cancer and was not expected to live much longer. In her despair, she said, "My mother died of cancer. I prayed every day of my life not to get cancer, and here I have it. What went wrong?" She was thinking to somehow blame God for her misfortune.

To her, our priest friend replied, "Woman, how could you help but get cancer? Your fear manifested it every day of your life. I would have been shocked if you did not get it." The woman's fear had produced the cancerous result as surely as if she was falling from a ladder to the ground. Like fighting against gravity itself, she plunged toward her fear.

Add to this the ever-mounting number of spontaneous remissions from cancer, arthritis, and multiple sclerosis without any medical treatment whatsoever. To this data add the thousands of drug research volunteers who are dismissed each year by pharmaceutical researchers for positive responses to placebos. Rather than tossing out this data, we are showing you that a human being's intentions can destructively interfere with negativity n our lives. The energy of the affliction simply cannot exist in the same universe as the energy out of phase with it. It is physically impossible. And, the opposite is also true. The affliction exists, because you have made a home for it with your own environment, whether you are conscious of it or not. Your parents, teachers, food, water, sunlight, as well as other people around you are an environment from which your genes choose specific proteins that make up every cell of your body, healthy or ill. There are only around 25 thousand genes in the human genome, and more than 120 thousand proteins. Each gene may have a choice of as many as 20 thousand proteins from which it can choose, based on your total environment. Once the cell is programmed with its phospholipid liquid crystal membrane, the program will run unconsciously, without change from the conscious mind. But, prior to forming that new cell, the mind is human intention is most definitely part of the total decision-making process of the genes.

We are not the product of our genetics, but rather the product of our environment. What I need you to realize is that you can modify your complete environment by your intention on the energy within you. And, when you change that, the environment around you cannot remain the same. In fact, it has already begun to change as soon as you realize you can change it. Imagine the effects you can have if you apply the power of your focused intention.

Like the light waves in Young's experiment, the energy from one person adds to the energy of another, and then another. If the energy resonates constructively, then that fear gains tremendous creative energy. What does it create? In the year 2015, after the great cataclysms of 2012 and 2013, the results of billions of people living in fear have been felt. The great wonders made with hands and minds of more than one hundred billion souls has come to ruin through the economic and shooting wars of a few managers of negative energy.

There is a small contingency of humanity that does not live in fear. Rather, they have a pure love about them. They see the good in one another. They are charitable and merciful and seek to grow life wherever they travel. The energy of these individuals also passes into the universe instantaneously. When they gather and resonate constructively, the effect is very positive and counteracts the negative power of fear-based energy. As it turns out, our studies have shown that because of the intention and focus of these positive energies, they are like a laser beam. That is to say, the energy is polarized and focused to a fine and powerful beam that has a targeted effect. Like a small amount of explosive applied at exactly the right place inside an old building, the positive energy generated by humans who are *awake* can clear a building to rubble in a few seconds that may have taken the energy of thousands of workers months to build. This clearing makes possible the construction of something new and beautiful and functional in place of something that was old and perhaps unsafe.

Most of these people are passive in nature. They are humble

105

and work many hours at employment, then save their money to buy a week of freedom to study or travel to places where they can share their peaceful natures with others. They are a cheek-turning people, accepting the aggression of others in a forgiving manner. They are easily taken advantage of by their employers, their neighbors, and even their governments. Throughout history, they have been forced to flee to the wilderness so they could have liberty from oppression. In the year 2015, there is no more wilderness.

Since the beginning of recorded time, these humble souls have blazed new trails across deserts, barren ice flows, oceans, mountains, and even into space. They sold everything they had for passage on a small wooden ship, or they pulled a handcart, or they indentured their lives and the lives of their children, so their grandchildren could live in freedom and liberty.

The result has been that the massive and chaotic power of fear has overcome the world. Like weeds, rapidly growing and ever consuming, never producing anything, the fear-based populace has shadowed every light and nearly wiped innocence from the Earth.

But there is hope. We discovered that fear has an allergy. We found that in the light, the dark energies of fear are cleared away. The challenge for us was to find a way to awaken and enlighten enough people in enough places around the world to flood the planet with light.

We discovered that when a person focuses their *attention* on something they want to accomplish, and then applies their *intention* toward making that manifest in the three-dimensional world, fear was replaced with love. Staying focused on the love, and not manifesting with one's fear, is the challenge of mortality. Teaching that one's attention could be consciously directed is powerful. Teaching how to master one's intention, was perhaps the most powerful lesson anyone could be taught. When people began to work the formulas of manifestation, the Earth began to change. Those methods were discovered thousands of years ago and lost or suppressed as leaders forced people to become dependent upon them for salvation and survival. They were rediscovered in the early 1990s and applied to a few people. The effect was almost good enough to change the course of humanity. Almost.

That is why we came back to the year 2010 to give you this book. We need the effect of awareness, enlightenment and conscious intention to be larger and more powerful earlier than our present conditions display. In other words, we need you to realize that you are a creator and that you can affect the universe with your intentions. We need you to do that in your day.

We need people to focus their attention and muster their intention to manifest the most beautiful paradise in all of the cosmos, right here on Earth. That is why we have worked so hard to return to begin the Spirit Race in March of 2010. There is a huge difference between what we are asking you to do and what other leaders or prophets have asked you to do. In the past, you may have been told to relinquish your will to someone else's. Do not do that. We need you to realize that your will is the most powerful thing you have. It is the envy of the universe. Not all sentient beings have free will. I am asking you to realize that your life condition, and thus the condition of the world and the universe, is altered each moment by your intention and Life energy. You are one hundred percent responsible for that energy.

We are asking that you take responsibility for that energy and direct your will to the creation of a peaceful and prosperous world. We know you want to be prosperous. We know you want all peoples to be prosperous. We also know that you fear this is not so, nor can it be so. Your fear is preventing it from becoming a reality. We are asking you to master your fears and apply your will with all of your strength to loving yourself and then loving your neighbor.

We are about to teach you the tools you need to control your body, and then to reach your heart. When you are there, you will soon be able to see where you want to be and where you can apply your energy. First, we will teach you these four steps to ensure you are successful in working the Law of Attraction:

1. Formulate and direct your intention into the universe.

2. Listen for the resonance of the universe.

3. Apply your sequence energy at the exact moment for constructive interference.

4. Continue for at least eight iterations to reach the Golden Mean.

Ringing bell?
I heard you today,
Do I offer thanks
To the rope,
A passing wind,
Or my wish,
At this moment
To hear your sweet tone?

Chapter 5: Unlocking the Secret

What understanding and tools are needed for unlocking the Secret? How can the relationship between the behaviors of energies in the universe have anything to do with the state of a human being? How can the energy of one human being make a difference in the universe? What you are about to learn will empower you to change yourself. When you change yourself, everything you touch, love, or think about will change as well.

Generally speaking, there are two types of people in the universe. The first believes that he is acted upon by the universe. The second believes he acts upon the universe. Let's discuss the first type. A common misconception is that bad things or good things happen to a person based on their knack for being in the right place at the right time. The misconception that random dumb luck determines if someone is a success or a failure at life is engrained in this type of person. These are the same people who regularly buy Lottery tickets expecting to produce a *ctrl-alt-del* reset on their poor financial habits.

If a person has bad luck, they are poor and chronically in debt, moving from illness to illness and never tasting of the good things in life. They yell at their kids in the grocery store. They gossip and argue easily, refuse to forgive others, and seek remedy often in drugs or alcohol. They rarely draw the pity of others nor do they offer charity to anyone. They consider themselves to be humble, due to their circumstances, yet they harbor a pride rooted in resentment of those who have somehow won life's lottery. Somehow they become proud that their humble.

If a person has good luck, they take family vacations every year. They drive new cars that are paid for. They start and succeed at businesses, sometimes selling their added value in those businesses for a profit. They are generally happy and well dressed. They love to meet people, travel, and forgive others easily. Their children all go to college, marry in storybooks, and have ne'er a weed in their perfectly manicured lawns. They go to church every Sunday, reach out and help others, cheerfully without thanks or recognition. They smile at and greet strangers, sing songs, and fuel the hobby and leisure industries with billions of dollars each year. They dream and follow those dreams, receiving great satisfaction and joy from that pursuit.

Now, let's discuss the second type of person, those who believe they act upon the universe. Many outside observers might not observe these individuals at first. These beings may be living in poverty or they may be wealthy. They may be leaders of large corporations or street artists. The key attribute is the knowledge they hold that they are affecting the universe on purpose. The idea that one is *on purpose* brings more fulfillment than all the wealth and human association imaginable. We will elaborate on this for you later.

When surveying people, I provided a question with multiple choices. Here are the question and the choices:

If you were to choose the result from a five-sided die (an idea originated by Ken Payne), which would you say more closely describes your life in its current state:

Side 1: My Current Life Condition is determined one hundred percent by destiny.

Side 2: My Current Life Condition is determined seventy percent by destiny and thirty percent by choice.

Side 3: My Current Life Condition is determined fifty percent by destiny and fifty percent by choice.

Side 4: My Current Life Condition is determined thirty percent by destiny and seventy percent by choice.

Side 5: My Current Life Condition is determined by my choices.

These surveys are conducted verbally. The reason they are conducted in this fashion is so the *energy* with which a person answers can be observed as well as the choice. When a person chooses Side 1, he invariably adds energy with his voice. When a person believes that nothing he thinks, says, or does has any effect on the current state of his life, it is reflected in the energy of his voice. That energy can contain hopelessness, as though surrendering to the inevitable course of the Earth around the sun. It may contain bitterness and resentment toward some force, spouse, parent, or even government. This person may not have love for himself. The energy is passionate, but directed outward toward everything that has been working against him. I have often heard statements like, "Every time I get to certain point, something always comes up to ruin everything." Even in this display

111

of energy, there is promise. The very fact that this person will add energy to the answer, belies a deep albeit sometimes flickering desire to rise out of that soul-poverty.

This energy transfers to the very dream they trying to accomplish, forcing it into failure. The fear of reprisal, rejection, or the suspicion that someone is going to steal your idea resonates with the universe to create the very thing you fear.

The person who chooses Side 2, Side 3, or Side 4 still does not understand the power they have in their being. Even more than the person who chooses a full-destiny answer, there is hope that the truth will set them free. This person realizes that his choices do affect the universe. He knows that he exists, and that his presence on the Earth changes the planet and the society, even if it is only very slightly. They may never write a book, or lead a company. They may never make a speech or even know how to read and write. They do, however, know they affect the universe when the look out over the family reunion and see the progeny of their love for their spouse. They see the bright children, or the one who teaches school, or the one who sings, or the twins who will someday be doctors.

Still, they harbor this idea that some power is out there stirring the pot for them. Some god or devil is walking beside him, knocking over his stack of cards, or breaking down his car, He somehow knows when he has saved a few dollars and reaches into his bag of tricks for an invoice that almost exactly matches the money in the bank.

The only other choice to consider is the one that reveals that the quality and conditions of a person's life are completely the result of personal choices. This realization is a huge jump from the destiny choices. It has been written, "Many are called, but few there be that are chosen."

In my opinion, *this is incorrectly translated.* The true statement should read, "**Many are called but few choose.**" The discovery that *we* are the total creators of our lives is the most important awakening of a person's life. This is the point at that "full responsibility" empowers the soul to reach its full potential. And this potential is absolutely unlimited. It is a shock at first.

"There is no way I chose to be sick," is a common answer I hear during the survey. "Do you think I like being poor and having nothing? You think I chose this for myself? Why in God's name would I do that?" The energy on these words is defiant and proud, even in the humblest of settings.

Full responsibility is extremely important, so we want to make sure you understand this point. We are not talking about duty, where one goes through the motions of life because of expectations for performance. Duty is a poor and misguided substitute for responsibility. Scripted by churches, governments, and even scientists, duty is a form of indoctrination of the most diabolical nature. Extremes for duty are easy and too numerous to mention.

During the presidential years—those years before the North American presidential council was put in place to stabilize world politics—there was a religion that was utilized to indoctrinate young children to become human bombers. As toddlers these innocents were taught to be Trojan horses. The tactic was known as terror. This form of duty was so terrible and so shocking to the world that three wars were fought to free the people from these religious tyrants. The duty placed upon children to die for the cowards who sought only death and mayhem was the most horrific crime against the soul since Satan drew a third of the host of heaven out into darkness with him.

When a human surrenders his sovereignty to another, he is already dead. When you raise your right hand and swear allegiance to any cause, leader, or creed, you have given someone else the power to control your life. Of course, you can choose to die. You can choose to trust another for your abundance. When a woman gives up her dreams to marry a man who does not let her develop and grow, she has traded a home and sex for her sovereignty.

The other sense of duty is much less morose, but just as debilitating to the development of a soul. Mostly perpetrated by religions, people are taught that they must sacrifice everything in order to be saved from eternal damnation. They are taught that giving up their own happiness and dreams for the good of someone else is the road to eternal life. They routinely use the life of Jesus as an example of this sacrifice. They focus on the crucifixion of Jesus, rather than the resurrection. They focus on the poverty and sad countenance in their carvings, paintings, and stories. They focus on the mortal misery and death of this great soul, and refuse to teach the real lessons he taught with his life. They teach that heaven can only be yours after a lifetime of suffering and misery, born with a smile and complete loyalty to the church.

Jesus' genuine teachings all rested on two things and only two things. Upon these two points of guidance rest all the commandments and all the laws that the universe recognizes.

I was asked by a caller during a globally broadcast radio interview on *The Kevin Smith Show* if I was a Christian. I responded by asking the caller, "What is a Christian?" I am sure the host had many hundreds of guests on his program over the years, and that he never got this question asked on his program. He was momentarily dumbfounded when he stepped in for the equally silent caller and said, "Well, that is someone who believes in Christ."

"This cannot be," I responded smoothly. "...For even the devils to believe and tremble." I quoted. "Surely devils are not Christians."

"Well, how would you define a Christian?" the host asked.

"I would say that someone who emulates Christ and seeks to act like Christ in his daily life, even when he is alone, is a Christian. In this case, I would say that I am a Christian."

Clearly, this was a good exchange for all of us. "That is the best definition I have ever heard," he said with a supportive tone.

Now, I am going to show you something here. There is actually a very nice deductive syllogism here. The words of Jesus' two greatest commandments were originally written in Greek in the ancient manuscript. By whom, we do not know. Perhaps this, along with most of the New Testament, was written by the Piso family. Perhaps it was actually said. Perhaps not. Truth is truth, however. It is written that Jesus said, "Love the Lord thy God with all thy heart, might, mind and strength. And the second is like unto it. Love thy neighbor as thyself." If you will open your mind for a moment I will show you this string of Greek logic. The conclusion was written first, then the premises in reverse order. This is very typical of the way Greek is translated into English. Many languages place the sentence in reverse order from English.

Logic would lay out a deductive syllogism to say, "If this premise is true, and this premise is true, then that is true conclusion." One must be sure the premises are true. Any high school Sophomore can recite to you a common geometrical proof that proceeds the same way. For example, if a shape is two-dimensional shape, and if the sum all interior angles of are 180 degrees, then that shape is a triangle.

Unraveling Jesus' logic statement, it reads like this. "If you love yourself, and if you can then love your neighbor as yourself, then you love God with all your heart might mind and strength."

The fact that love is the most powerful creative energy in the universe is the one lesson we wish you to retain from this work. I am not talking about affection only, or about infatuation, or even about lust or sex. We are sharing the love one might have for his work, or for his soul mate, or even for playing or listening to music. We are talking about the self-centered flow of energy that does not sacrifice the self for anything or anyone. That is a deception. The giving of one's self is

116

the greatest gift in the universe. But this is a joyful giving. Anyone who comes before you crying and says, "I gave you everything. I gave you the best years of my life. I treated you like a son. And you repay me like this?" has shown their pride and their arrogance and just how little they thought of you. The energy is dark and negative, as was the motivation behind their giving in the first place. The resent you. They most certainly do not love you, but rather they love the way it made them appear as they pretended to love you. No good can ever come from sacrificing. It is only joyful giving with no expectation that can create.

There is joy that accompanies this kind of love that will not allow violence to exist. It will only allow growth and peace. In response to love this powerful, energy will manifest into matter itself by its own free will and choice.

This love is the creative power to which mountains will move themselves and around which planets will orbit. When one person gives this love for or to another person, both souls will feel valuable and glorious.

There are many ways by which this kind of love can exist in each of us. Notice that I am not saying that this love can be *possessed* by anyone. This love exists as a vibration that raises the soul to a new level. This vibration is the Life energy of the individual. Trying to grip this love with the intention of never letting it go, is like trying to grip water in the hand. Only gently cupping the water will retain it.

117

Trying to hold onto love is like trying to hold onto air in your lungs by holding your breath. If you do this too long, you will pass out and fall and break something. Not really. You can't hold your own breath until you pass out. But, you get the point. The air must be exchanged and given back to the world while taking in the freshness of love from the plants or algae that cleaned the air for you to breathe. The freedom that you afforded the air is the same freedom you provide love. It goes out, and without fear it will return to you if, and only if, it is the choice of the love and your choice to receive it. It is a little difficult to command someone to receive something, but if it was possible then this is one you should consider following.

When this Life energy is raised to a high enough level, full awareness occurs, and the individual now has a new attention level. Energizing this Life energy higher in frequency is our intention. We want you to focus your intention on raising your frequency through intention. If you can do this, you will manifest a higher consciousness. The righteousness described by those ancient writers is nothing more than the continuous correction through internal feedback to achieve Christ consciousness.

A few people have felt this kind of consciousness in their lives and know what it feels like. They have also been able to overcome the challenges of life because they were able to send out the positive energy it took to manifest success.

Most people do not have this experience. They are generally unaware of the energies around them, feeling instead like their lives are the result of chance or even worse, that of destiny.

The reality is that they have mirrors or blockages in their individual flow of Life energy. They have had past events in their lives that create eddy fields in their Life energy that result in repeating errors and preventing success. This is the primary reason why people are not able to unlock the secret of the Law of Attraction.

The Law of Attraction exists and functions for all conscious beings. *All entities have consciousness. They are not all, however, conscious that they are conscious.* Nevertheless, they work the law all the same, some to their benefit and thus the benefit of the universe, and some to the destruction of themselves and those around them. They do not see out of their own eyes with purpose. They are deep inside of their bodies, controlled by them, and wielded by them like wild animals. They are slaves to forces in the third dimension, such as lust of the flesh, the lust of the eye, and the pride of life.

There are those few who are conscious that they are conscious. There are more intelligences stepping into their beings every day. These intelligences are more inspired by *being* than they are by *having*. They are functioning by *doing* those activities that develop their being rather than by *doing* those activities that gain them things. There is a massive difference in the energy of these people. They are changing themselves, their relationships with one another, and they are changing the universe on purpose.

Of course, the reason we are sending this book back to you in the year 2010 is because not enough people were able to operate this law for positive. They lost hope, which a major was a setback for the planet of human beings. We are trying to prevent this setback from occurring. You are the key to accomplishing this. But you are unable to do it on your own.

I discovered in the future, and I hope not too late, this very special key to unlocking the secret of the Law of Attraction. People need to have a clear path for their Life energy to flow without their own future threads forming a sticky web that prevents the bounty from reaching through. The vast majority of people cannot clear their own way through the baggage and patterns of their past lives. How far past can that be?

Well, that is a powerful threshold for people to cross. The truth is that not all beings have mortal human lives past this experience on Earth. They have no history to carry forward. That does not mean they do not have experiences or lessons

Ok. This is probably a good place to talk about soul wounds. Every soul encounters challenges that cause pain. This can come in the form of the death of a loved one, the loss of a job, or merely the realization that one did not achieved a dream. It can come from harm that we have done to another soul. It can come from divorce or the heartbreak of a lost relationship. It can come from war, oppression, and slavery. The victims of ancient cities were able to manifest fire and brimstone with their cries for vengeance.

There is a dual cycle of human social groups that has never been broken. It can be broken, but it will take the conscious intention of masters of Life energy to accomplish it. The cycle looks like the graphic below:

The cycle begins anywhere you like, but works like this. If you begin at Mercy, then the result is Peace. When we are forgiving and watch out for the welfare of the many, then there is peace in the land. The people prosper and become wealthy together, without guile or jealousy. People live by the laws of love and look for good in all beings and help that good to grow.

Sooner or later, leadership takes a strange twist. The people raise someone up who is willing to take on responsibility as a public servant. They feel the power of using the prosperity of others to do great things. Then the lust for power set in. About the same time, the people ask for this person to take over the responsibility of protecting society from competitors. Laws are enacted. People break the laws. The public trust demands protection from the lawbreakers. Perhaps, instead of forgiving and loving people to help them grow and realize their mistakes, they begin to administer justice. At first it is a few. Then it becomes a minority. Then it becomes a majority.

Mercy gives way to Justice, and the next the next cycle begins. As soon as someone demands justice, the call for war is forthcoming. Borders are enforced; resources are hoarded and dedicated to building up the central powers that protect the people from harm. Then the central powers become their own nation, demanding their own support and never wanting to give up their job. They get good at it. That means enemies must get good at it as well. Then the factories that sell and outsmart the weapons of both sides make money and attract their own secret resources. You get the picture of where we are in the year 2015?

121

Souls can suffer harm from sacrifice and from fear. Very few people can clear a soul wound on their own. Most people recover from the event and build a wall around that event in their souls. Like a cyst, it sits there invisible to our defense system and never leaves. When the time comes for us to make a choice about something, or react to some stressful event, the encysted soul wound taints the Life energy again and again. It seems as though the person can never overcome this pattern. And, unless the soul wound is cleared they will never move beyond that point in this life, or perhaps in subsequent lives as well. That clearing must be done by someone who is trained in the science of discovery and soul *cystectomies*.

Full Life energy flow is the key to unlocking the secret. *Clearing* is the vital process for helping a person's Life energy to flow. Once this Life Energy can flow without the blockages from old habits, patterns, and other subconscious scripts, the failures that seem to repeat themselves will melt away.

Keep in mind that these patterns can come from many sources. They can be scripted from your parents, your teachers, your friends, and even from enemies. These are memorized by the cell membranes of your body. You react with defensive methods on a cellular level that is beyond reach of your conscious mind. In fact, the mind is normally as detached from your consciousness as your reflexive knee is to the physician's rubber mallet. What you are about to learn is how to get your conscious sentient mind reconnected to your subconscious by creating a safe and positive presence in your heart. You will learn how to get in your own heart-mind.

Through this process you can follow a future path that simply was not available to you in your negative energy state. The mathematics and physics of this process will be explained so you can understand it, not just so that it makes this book sound *scientific* and glittery with fancy terms. You will know for yourself how to open your future to the potential of all potentialities. Here we go.

Memories;
Quantum foam of intention
From that roars the Present
For one fleeting moment,
Reminisced, lamented, treasured
Notes in a symphony called Creation.

Chapter 6: Tapping at the Right Time

In this chapter, I am going to teach you the Phoenix Sequence. The discovery of the mathematical process by which human intention can be applied to create a resonant increase of power is *the Secret*. This is the process by which the Law of Attraction works. I mean it actually functions like a formula that cannot fail. Nikola Tesla discovered that a tiny amount on energy, applied at exactly the right moment, can not only overcome the inertia – that is the resistance to movement – of huge bridges and buildings, it can move Life energy as well.

We have been building a foundation of knowledge and experience so that you will understand the process I am about to explain to you. It is simple, and in that simplicity it is genius. Are you ready to learn why and how the Law of Attraction really works? Okay, here we go.

Humans are sophisticated and cunning. They are self-preserving at all costs and nearly always react to their surroundings rather than change their surroundings to suit their desires. How do you think an animal with slow muscles, no body hair to speak of, poor hearing, no night vision, and no claws of any kind could survive on a harsh planet like Earth? Human *beings* are defined as those humans who are in some stage of awareness that he or she has existed before and will exist long after this life. Many traditions teach of this, and many do teach the concept of pre-Earth lives. Yet this early life is believed to be in the form of a spirit without physical form, as if we came from some sort of *Guf* (also Gup or Guph: The Well of Souls) where all spirits await their one shot at mortality to add to the processing of their intelligence from some sort of god-thought-embryo into a full-fledged god with all power and knowledge. This is nearly completely, and almost certainly, utter nonsense.

You most certainly have existed for eons. In fact, you have existed from the beginning with *source*. You may be one of the Old Ones who can recall more clearly your experience and wisdom. You may be one of the Young Ones, who have barely the memory of being born in this lifetime. There are those who would claim that your awareness of your experiences on other worlds, in far away lifetimes, has no bearing on your life here even if it was true. Nothing could be further from the truth. You presence here, along with the other billions of sentient souls here, is exactly the point. It wasn't random. It was by choice. Your choice. Don't think for one moment beyond this sentence that your choice to come here, either freshly in this lifetime or in many lifetimes here, is without purpose or importance. You are part of a live and conscious population of sentient beings that is here precisely because this rare and beautiful planet is about to go through a metamorphosis, an evolution, to which your specific frequency adds to the vibration of this event.

Watching this event from the other side of the universe would hardly be the spot to observe this amazing event. There are stars

125

visible from Earth. Around these stars there are planets. Some of those planets are capable of supporting human life on the surface, but not many. And of those planets, not one near a visible star is at the stage in evolution that this one currently enjoys. You came here to stop her death by the locust-mentality. You came here to lift her and join her in this change, and through doing so you too will evolve in a mighty leap. That's exactly why you were born here and exactly why so many races are traveling here from other worlds. They want what you have by birth; a chance to experience the live birth of a new world. This embryo Earth needs eternal souls to accompany her through the veil of dimensions. You are among the only ones who are capable of doing that. In fact, some of you have done it before on other worlds. That is why you feel so out of place here. That is why you do not seek wealth and material goods, but rather seek love and to lift others to a state of love.

There are those in your time who speak of these great changes with a fearful message. "You will be destitute," they whine. "There is no time to follow love. The time is to prepare for poverty and devastation," they scream as they offer their workshops and shelters and irrevocable words of God.

I am not saying these times will be like anything you have ever seen in your mortality here on Earth. I am not saying there won't be systemic upset, cataclysms, and perhaps even economic meltdown. I am saying when you're awake and cognizant of who you really are, that it won't matter. I am saying that wealth and estates and fine furniture and gold will be meaningless to you in the presence of your

126

powerful love for one another. Remaining mortal isn't the purpose of life, my fellow Earth explorers. Being in love, being merciful, and learning everything you can while you are here with a song on your lips and an open hand to others is closer to the message we have been trying to share with you. And when the time comes, and rest assured it will happen exactly when it supposed to happen, you will add exactly what it needed to the symphony of the Earth's trans-dimensional shift. If you're here reading this book, you just had a feeling that you will go through it with her. You are one of the planetary midwives, as it were.

The awakened human being realizes he or she has mortal experiences well beyond the ones from this life. These are not merely déjà vu, or the channeling of some other being's thoughts, or even the co-existent entanglement of your three-dimensional self with another model of your intelligence that exists in another universe, or dimension, or on this Earth.

There is no *god-construct* around which all of us sit like huge super-computers, imaging our many peripheral mortalities through life-force modems. The idea that life is for the entertainment of some god, or that it is some kind of punishment for tasting apples, or that we are genetic beasts of burden who became self-aware and got away from our task masters is irrelevant. There is no all-powerful being sitting out there in space that sends people to hell or delivers them to mansions in the sky with scores of virgins to attend to their needs. These stories may have been formed by the very governing religions that used their exclusive access to *truth* as a sledgehammer to crush those who spoke of the intuition they were receiving from the *source* energy that exists around all of us.

The truth is that we judge ourselves and condemn ourselves to our own next life by the vibrations we originate. A *sin* is nothing more than missing the target. Try again and improve your aim. There is no joy in not being able to hit what you are aiming for. For good or ill, the focus of our energy is ours to wield. The responsibility for those vibrations, the life energy of our soul, is our responsibility and only our responsibility. Again, let us say that it does not matter how we are loved by others. It only matters how we love them. Everyone.

Each and every one of us is an individual with immense power and glory wrapped up inside. The sovereignty of that knowledge is the greatest key to freedom and creation in the universe. It may be exactly why the universe is expanding at an accelerated rate. But what is the source of existence? Where did you come from? Who are you? Hold onto something. You are about to hear the truth perhaps for the very first time.

Let's pick up things a picosecond after the beginning. Keep in mind that the Big Bang never happened. You, and I am speaking of the collective of sentient beings in the universe, are still inside the singularity of the original universe, but your love has created time by speeding it up from the zero of the speed of light.

The original Source was unaware. It was alone in the void. It was void because the void was not awake, but rather snoozing in bliss. That's simple enough. There was no up or down or left or right, because there was nothing but blackness everywhere. Or perhaps there was nothing but light everywhere. Either way, there was no horizon, no hill or dale or ripple anywhere.

Then an amazing thing happened. Source awakened its attention and realized it was asleep and alone and void. This *attention* is a most important concept to master. It is the first mark of sentience. The moment an intelligence can say, "I am," is the moment it realizes, "*I am* is god." Yes.

Attention is the act of a being becoming aware that it is observing something. That observation usually begins with one's self. We might look at our own feet a million times as an infant, but the first time we wonder at their shape, color and texture and movement is an amazing experience. Watch an infant the day he discovers his own feet. He'll reach for them, all out of control and flailing like some sort of robot controlled by a panel with unmarked buttons. Watching the infant punch all the buttons on the arm and leg control panel as he tries to learn how to capture that lovely five-toed object out there in plain sight is a fascinating exercise. The closer they get to associating their proximity sensors and the calcium-fired biotics that make the arms and legs move, the more excited these babies become.

Until, at long last, they capture the ever-elusive foot with one reflexive grasp. Then a very strange thing happens. They nearly stop all movement. The quadriceps and calf muscles relax. The biceps and forearm muscles work together like a rod and reel to pull the foot in for a closer viewing. And then the amazing thing happens. The foot is drawn into the orifice, the mouth, in which are placed the two most amazing biological spectrometers in the universe. The tongue is a nearly perfect atomic force microscope able to discern very fine details in texture and composition. Upon it are millions of sensors able to perform molecular analysis to a few parts in one million. Salty, sweet, bitter, and sour aspects can be assessed in infinite combinations at blinding speed and to absolutely quantitative precision.

The addition of the nose brings the most powerful and unmistakable piece of analytical equipment in the universe into play. It is the single most powerful means of identity in existence. Once a molecule has been sensed with the average nose, it is permanently cataloged in the memory of that intelligence. Whatever has been associated with that smell is committed to permanent memory.

The infant is now self-aware of the foot. In a few days, he or she will be able to command that foot to its mouth for another examination, until the brain is satisfied it knows everything it wants to know about the foot, and the method for bringing it to the mouth. Depending on the boredom level reached with this new discovery, and perhaps fueled by the success event of completing the analysis of the foot, the infant will move on the next item to be examined. Every single item picked up by this infant will be placed directly into the mouth for complete scanning.

And within a year or so, the eyes will take over as sole sensor for most objects. Energy in the form of light will take over as the rational form of negotiating one's way around the universe. The mouth and tongue are rarely used for close examination of much more than food or another human body after this point. Perhaps this comes from the hand being slapped away from the mouth by parents, or perhaps it is the result of a bad experience of something being placed into the mouth. Something too hot, cold, bitter, or just plain nasty-tasting will begin the process of using the eyes and nose for non-destructive analysis in advance of placing something into the mouth. It is a complex set of lessons that can be part of even more complex cultures and customs involving the palate and available sources of food. But now you have the idea of how amazing the beginning of self-awareness can be.

Awareness is the first defining characteristic between a human and a human being. A human may be an amazing and complex animal with speed and coordination and an undeniably robust drive to procreate and preserve its own life. But, it is an animal nonetheless. A human is brutal and violent and ever consuming of its environment. It hunts, and gathers, and mates, and will kill competitors to any of those activities. It lives on rage and lust and greed, and will watch another human starve to death without lifting a finger to teach it how to survive if it thinks for a moment that there is not enough to share. It will dig a pit for its neighbor and breathe a sigh of good riddance as the homeless are relocated to the morgue.

A human *being* is the most amazing combination of spiritual and temporal energies in the universe. A human being is the most glorious awareness and is a fascination for all other beings in the universe. The awareness of a being is often called consciousness. When humans exhibit higher consciousness, all other beings in the universe pay close attention.

A human being works in harmony with other life forms. It manages resources at all levels. A human being is not only self-aware, it is aware of all other life in its environment. At this point, we can stop calling a human being *it* and start calling a human being *he*. This is no disrespect to the female of the species. It is merely for simplicity in writing. If you are a woman receiving this book, please mentally replace the word *he* with *she*.

A human being realizes that for his life to continue, some other life form must be consumed. On the most basic level, grass or carrots or algae are consumed by simple life forms. Higher and higher the consumption continues as minerals build plants, and plants build animals, and animals build animals. A human being is aware of this entire ecology and seeks to maintain the balance between all these things. He is aware of the beauty and design of nature. He sees that bees pollinate the flowers, which give rise to fruit that may sustain his life. So, he manages the bees along with his fruit trees.

He is aware that fresh water falls from the sky and fills lakes, rivers, and streams, and is the liquid of life. So he manages the lakes and rivers and streams and oceans of the world so that they are not polluted or obstructed or lost to deserts. He may fish from them, but not take all the fish. He may irrigate his garden, but not consume all the water or pollute the river to prevent his neighbor from also watering his garden. And if there is not enough water, then he learns to collect and gather the rain and manage that resource so everyone can have some.

He is also aware that he is not the only sentient being in the universe. He can learn to freely communicate with beings from all worlds, times, and even universes. He is sensitive to the desires of others and seeks to make things better for others whenever he can. He plays with the cetaceans with the same joy he would any intelligent species in the universe. He may not even domesticate animals for consumption, because he reveres life so much that he cannot fathom one life ending so another can live. Although the feelings of a cabbage can be argued, he has no compunction for consuming copious quantities of sauerkraut. The microscopic life that feeds more complex life to sustain human life is an acceptable and comfortable component to the equation, and he is ever grateful for the bounty of that arrangement.

Let us get back now the idea of *attention*. The awakened human being realizes he has mortal experiences well beyond the present one. There is wisdom in not living in the past, but a working knowledge of these lives may clear patterns of behavior that enable the *being* to reach immortality.

We need to be very clear that the rules of observation always apply. The observation effect is an advanced process of awareness. The observation of past events will change them. The past is an infinite asymptotic tube not unlike an ice cream cone. The singularity at the end is the point of Source division. Let me explain.

The point of *I am* is the point of Source.

$\bigcirc$ = Void

There is no attention. There is only Source or *self.* There is no up, down, inside, or outside. There is no awareness. There are only self and sleep and bliss.

$$\sqrt{SOURCE} = \Phi = \textbf{I am}$$

Source (Self) becomes aware. In this awakening, self shouts, "I am," and bursts into existence.

Although Self is aware, there is still not perspective. The function must be run to completion. The most difficult action in creation now has to occur. Self has to free itself from the bounds of its Source. It must somehow divide the source-circle and allow the function to happen. But this is not a division like a cell divides in two. The process is actually the square root of Source. That means that the two beings multiplied by each other are Source. In fact, all of us times each other are Source. We cannot be separated from the equation. It is in us, and we are in it. The square root is released into the universe as two soul mates. .

Φ x Intention = OO

The application of intention to Phi is the creative force. There is now perspective, because in this square root function, Source becomes two. Now there is distance and there is some other intelligence with whom to share existence. This other entity is identical in every way to the other, except that one is female and one is male. One is yin and one is yang. When they swirl around each other, creation continues to happen. One can never exist without the other, and would simply collapse into Source again without perspective and lost in the bliss of the void.

This love and mating is so powerful that it is the creative force for the entire universe. Source is God, and God is you. That is to say, when the two parts are multiplied together, aware and loving and in love, creation occurs. The variety of life in the sea, the sky, and the very energy in the universe itself are the result of the creative force of all the source intelligences in the universe agreeing to create.

When the two parts become separated by space and time, they experience mortality separately, growing and aching for one another. This is also part of the growth process. One would think that gods know everything, are omni-prescient, but intimate knowledge of the third dimension is so powerful and so integral to the love that they keep coming back over and over again to either gain it for themselves, or act as a teacher and mentor to others so they experience this joy at least once in their existence. You know who you are. If you feel a little out of place in this world, perhaps with an acute sensitivity for man's inhumanity, then it's possible you are from this clan of newcomers to the Earth.

These gods are ever seeking one another throughout the universe, being born and expiring over and over again on one world and then another. When they find one another – and the recognition can take place over great distances in a flashing appearance – the joy is so powerful that every sentient being in the universe and throughout all dimensions rejoices. If you have felt that feeling it is quite amazing. If you haven't, watch for it when you begin to increase your circle of acquaintances. They're out there, and they are looking for you too.

Ascended masters from all dimensions may come to herald the event, and it is a sight to behold.

The presence of these ascended masters has been photographed. *Orbs* can be photographed with digital or film-type cameras with or without a flash. These also can be observed with the naked eye, but the vibrational level of the observer must be raised to be able to detect the energy. Like ultraviolet radiation, it is just out of the frequency band for the human cells in the eye. With proper preparation, the cells can become sensitive to this radiation and see them appear. *Orbs* appear in all sizes and colors. The designs in them are not unlike the mandalas recreated by Tibetan monks in sand or with their artwork. The more high-resolution the camera, the easier it is to see the designs inside the *orb*. I have observed veritable rivers of orbs flowing through crowds of people, when viewing the surroundings through infrared goggles while the area is being flooded with infrared light.

Orbs are attracted to love. Numerous experiments conducted by the author have proven that *orbs* can be nowhere in sight after numerous camera shots. However, upon applying a loving intention to the area, subsequent shots reveal *orbs* appearing in large numbers.

In one such experiment, a high-resolution digital camera was set on a tripod at night in the center of a large group of observers. The reason this experiment is inserted at this point is because the feeling of remembrance and recognition is one that should be felt and should be used as a guide as we proceed with this training.

The camera was set to take a picture every ten seconds for one minute; six shots in total. The author's friend, Miceal Ledwith (author of *The Orb Project*), stood in an Echinacea field in the dark of night with his hands down at his sides while maintaining a blank and neutral mind. The first flash occurred. He then raised his arms above his head as if beholding the stars over head and began to extend his love into the area. He was almost in an act of blessing. The second flash occurred. He continued to extend his intention for loving the people watching him in a large circle around him, as well as the space around him. The third and fourth flashes occurred. He then lowered his hands and began to return his mind to the neutral and blank state with that he began. The fifth and sixth flashes occurred.

We then went inside to a meeting hall, and the camera was connected to a computer that was connected to a projector. The images were put on the wall in sequence. In the first picture, Miceal was seen alone in the blackness around him. There were no bugs, as it was about fifty degrees Fahrenheit, and there was no breeze of any kind blowing. In the second picture, Miceal is observed with his arms above his head, and a white mist is beginning to form around him as if being conjured between his upraised arms.

In the third picture the mist is so think that it nearly obscures his face. The appearance of *orbs* is profound. There are about a dozen of them in blue, red, white, lavender, green, and even pink. In the third picture, the mist is so thick, Miceal cannot even be seen from the waist up. There are hundreds of *orbs* of nearly every color in the rainbow. In the fourth picture the mist takes on the form of a vortex or a tornado while the *orbs* are too numerous to count. Perhaps there were a thousand of them.

In the fifth and sixth pictures, the mist is dissipating and the *orbs* can be seen exiting the area, as if cooperating with the demonstration. Now, here is the remarkable thing. The camera was a ten-megapixel camera with a large lens and an external flash. The resulting detail in these shots was extremely fine. When these were shown on the wall of the meeting hall, the image was perhaps sixteen feet across. One could walk up to the *orb* displayed on the wall and observe the patterns inside the *orbs*. There were horses, men with beards sitting in lotus position, schematics, geometric patterns, and even what looked like complex machines displayed in clear detail in many of the *orbs*. No two were alike. This was a controlled and objectively observed experiment. The results were irrefutable. The *orbs* appeared as the result of loving intention, were not a flaw in the camera, nor were they the result of dust or insects in the air. One could only wonder how unaware we normally are of the presence of beings that are drawn to our love. The feelings that were recognized by the observers of this experiment were powerful and wonderful.

The reason this is a square root function is simple enough. The circumference of a circle is calculated by using π and multiplying the radius of that circle by itself. The circle gets larger as the square of its radius multiplied by π (pi). This becomes even more fantastic as one realizes that the future, emanating from this Source Point forward, is shaped like a cone and not circle. The volume of the cone represents the potential of all potentialities.

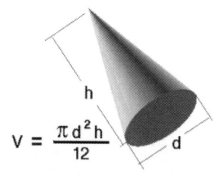

$$V = \frac{\pi d^2 h}{12}$$

Fig. 12. The square root function occurs because of expansion in all directions at once as the potential of all potentialities.

This is the result of a two-dimensional circle moving through space with an increasing diameter. Each moment in time is a circle, but the function fits so closely together in such an immediate sequence that it forms a cone. The sides of the cone should be straight, but they rarely are because of future threads. What's a future thread? I am glad you asked. We're going to cover that in better detail when we discuss dreams, but here is the idea.

When we put an dream out there in the future, we often tend to make a, "but-first list." I don't mean you walk backwards. I mean we have a habit of planning *how* we are going to get there; by saying, "...but first I have to do this, and first I have to do that..." We tell the universe how we are going to get there. Unfortunately, that thread of events rarely resonates with the available energy in the universe, and so the dream is rarely realized. What happens to the perfect cone is that it becomes rather shaped a little like a tornado, twisting and writhing into the future with power and glory, yet always increasing in radius. The entire structure of one's time life is always changing, and thus difficult to compute, but one can see from the parabolic cone section below that each segment is observable.

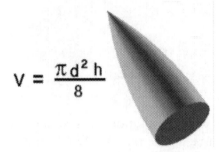

$$V = \frac{\pi d^2 h}{8}$$

Fig. 13. The changing volume of the cone over time is a result of human intention changing the denominator in the formula.

Do you see what happened to the formula? The denominator changed. We change it by reducing the possibilities, the potentials, of the universe. We may squeeze it down with our own ego to a single line of possibility by forcing the universe into a process it cannot support, thus blocking the very abundance the universe has in store for us.

As the future is traced back to the present's event horizon, the past narrows to the region around the thread. As the thread is observed, the other dimensions around that thread are affected as well. There are fields within fields and nuances of fact and metaphysics that can be observed and therefore changed by the human being. Segments of the *tornado* or cone can be observed by themselves, which can make working the process more simple. Normally, review of one's past is not done back to the moment of birth. There is a membrane, a veil, and there are disconnects between the very young being and the being that is self-aware. I call this process *stepping in*. A very old being who has been born into a new body has nothing in common with the little child. He or she wants to be adult and think adult and get back to whatever what was left undone in the life before. But the very young child body often does not want to cooperate. Beethoven and Liszt resumed playing the piano as prodigal ages. Artists draw, mathematicians calculate, and other amazing gifts burst through tiny bodies to make great contributions, but make no mistake here. The very passionate being will feign to step into a small body and be a child. The typical age is around nine years of age when the light goes on. Sometimes the connection is lost through a variety of conditions, which may or may not be the choice of the child, but the general rule is that the more that must be overcome in order to come of age, the greater the potential of accomplishment the being may realize. No true leader was ever born into the lap of luxury. There is no advantage of beauty, strength, or even intelligence. I know failures with each and all of these traits. There is only one thing that yields a legacy. That one thing is determination. You don't need eyesight, legs, or even the ability to speak to become greater than your imagination. Determine to work this formula, and you cannot fail. The entire universe will shake at your intention and spontaneously yield forth its abundance if you learn these points and apply what I am about to tell you.

The potential of all potentialities can be considered in small sections. We select sections of time to examine. This mathematically fits the past review process better than an entire cone formula. The thing to keep in mind is the relationship of events, and how the future possibilities expand in all directions as the square of the distance. The values in the equation are not necessary. The relationship between the different values is important. This structure is called a frustum.

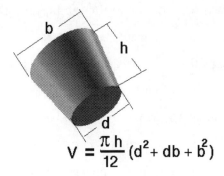

$$V = \frac{\pi h}{12} (d^2 + db + b^2)$$

Fig. 14. The frustum is a section of time examined from a starting line forward to a fixed future time.

Inside this multi-dimensional space, one has a tendency to force threads or pathways of intention into the future. Although represented by mathematical functions on strings, there are very real aspects of past threads that make up the fabric of past life, and thus of spacetime itself. The attention of a being on the past will entwine with the attention of other beings that may have been part of that experience. Even plants and microorganisms are eventually affected by the observation of a being placed upon a past thread. These past threads are real, yet each time they are observed, they are changed. Even random number generators, also called RNG's, can be altered in the past by the observation of a human being.

Traveling here without a guide can be done, but in order to safely and expeditiously clear an error in a past thread, it is recommended that a guide be utilized for the first few times. I recommend finding a clearing practitioner if you are suffering from life overwhelm, or the loss of some kind that brings you great sadness or weakness. Other than this, you can do it by yourself and realize awesome results. One of the key reasons for effectively observing the past is to correct the position of the present and create a pathway to the future from here. But, let's save the future pathway process for later. For now, just learn the ability to observe the past and effect constructive changes in the now.

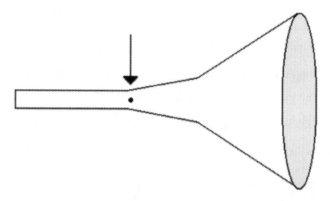

Fig. 15. The past has a narrow range of possibilities for new effects from intention. Self (the dot) can see forward or backward in time.

The Past-Cone is a three-dimensional cone that contains all the energy memories of all the actions, inactions, and interactions between them and everything else in the universe as it pertains to Self. The Past is not a straight line, but rather a narrow tube. It has a small range of possibilities, but there are still observations that can be made and lessons learned.

The immediate future is a narrower cone, because of the choices we have made up to this point. You may have chosen not to stay in school. You may have gotten married. You may have chosen not to save money or invest wisely. The slightly more distant future is wide open to the potential of all potentialities. That is, unless we force one of future threads into the future by dictating how dream will come to fruition. "I don't know," is an acceptable answer when it comes to knowing how the abundance will come. You'll know it when it occurs, believe me. The threads stretched toward you from the future are multi-dimensional.

Consider a single-filament fiber under a microscope. It is sort of like a one-photon thick wire. Even though the filament is exceedingly small, there is girth to the filament. That is to say, there is a cross-section, no matter how small it may be. This thread will be multidimensional having a wealth of energy and a specific sound that you are going to be trained to listen for.

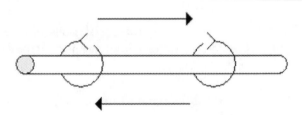

Fig 16. Future thread with four dimensions of possibilities

Now, there are two directions of consideration around each of these filaments in the fabric and two directions for flow: forward and reverse. There is a counter-clockwise and a clockwise direction. Each of these directions will have certain energy. Those energies are equal and opposite, because the thread is stable and contains all the information you need to hold your weight while it supports you. When they are combined exactly out of phase, the result is zero; therefore, only one direction can be considered at once. In other words, you have to make a choice when the moment comes to you.

When the MerKaBa is rotated with a net counterclockwise energy, there is a certain consideration and life is given to everything. When it is rotated with a net clockwise energy there is another consideration and everything planned or unplanned dies. This is why we are taught to rotate one complete star tetrahedron counterclockwise at a speed ratio of 34 and one complete star tetrahedron clockwise at a speed ratio of 21. These are not actual revolutions, but rather form a ratio of 34 to 21, and these are both numbers in the Fibonacci Sequence that we will discuss in a little further in the book. If we divide 34 by 21 we almost get a perfect Golden Mean at 1.619. The difference between the two numbers is a 13 counterclockwise motion of the entire MerKaBa which produces life. Each human being has three complete MerKaBa fields.

The primary one is motionless. It is oriented according to the predominant sex of the being. If the female energy is the predominant energy of the being, then the upper tetrahedron, called the Sky Tetrahedron, has the flat surface facing forward. If the predominant energy of the being is male, then the flat surface faces rearward.

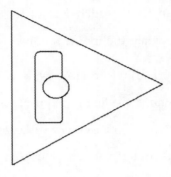

Fig. 17. The male sky tetrahedron orientation with the edge pointing forward. This is the upper tetrahedron attached to the physical body.

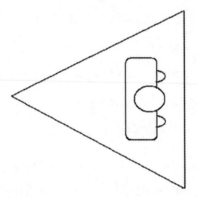

Fig. 18. The female sky tetrahedron orientation with the flat pointing forward. This is the upper tetrahedron attached to the physical body.

This orientation applies to the sexual orientation of the being no matter what the biological sex of the person might be. This energy field is normally symmetrical. It may be distorted if the being at some point in his or her life suffered emotional or physical trauma and never was cleared of that wound. Beings suffering from soul wounds or who are taking hallucinogenic drugs may not be able to maintain a symmetrical MerKaBa field. Keep in mind that this is only the physical portion of three MerKaBa fields that exist around the life energy axis of each human being.

The other two Star Tetrahedron fields are identical in size and shape, but there is a distinct difference. They rotate. All three Star Tetrahedrons are superimposed upon the other with precisely the same axis. Under normal circumstances, the female Star Tetrahedron field rotates counterclockwise, and the male Star Tetrahedron rotates clockwise. Remember, they cannot rotate at the same speeds in opposite directions. If this were to happen, the result would be zero.

It is for this reason that they rotate in that specific ratio. Now, here is the most important mathematical discovery with relation to the Law of Attraction and how to make it give forth its abundance.

The Phoenix Sequence

What you are about to learn is the most important key to unlocking *The Secret* of the Law of Attraction. It utilizes a mathematical process of increase that is found in nature by which order rises out of chaos. The sequence was discovered by an Italian mathematician named Leonardo Pisano, whose nickname was Fibonacci. While I was modifying one my previous lesson plans for my Algebra students at the college, I started playing with the Sequence with my calculator. I wanted to start somewhere other than zero, but I wanted to follow the same process. I entered two random numbers and added them together, and started from there. After only eight iterations, the last two numbers divided one into the other achieved the Golden Proportion of 1.618 to 1. This was a stunning discovery. I went at it for hours, using non-integers, fractions, and even imaginary numbers. It worked every time. I proved that any values, even energy of intention, increased in this way would achieve the Golden Proportion and be supported by the resonance rules of the Universe.

Fig. 19. Fibonacci is the nickname of Leonardo Pisano, the renowned Italian theorist of numbers.

Fibonacci was a brilliant mathematician who rediscovered the progression of growth in nature. We say rediscovered, because these growth progressions have been known for millions of years by all creators in the universe. Honey combs, sunflowers, pinecones, and even the ratio of the human face length to width as well as the hands to the arms and many other ratios are the result of this sequence of numbering.

It is very simple. The number sequence normally starts with zero, as does all creation. There are circumstances where Fibonacci relationships can arise out of other progressions, which we will explain in a moment. Here is a normal consideration for the first thirteen Fibonacci numbers:

0, 1, 1, 2, 3, 5, 8, 13, 21, 34, 55, 89, 144

Notice that the first two numbers are added together to get the third, and so forth along the number line. There is something even more amazing about these numbers. When the progression reaches the numbers 34 and 55, the following consecutive numbers form a very close proximity to the Golden Mean of 1.618 when divided into one another. This is where the curve goes away and the plotted line become rather straight at a very specific slope of 1.618. In other words, the standard deviation from the plotted line become very small and the line doesn't change slope except in the fourth decimal place.

In other words, when the number 55 is divided by 34 the result rounds to 1.619. <u>This is extremely important when considering creation.</u> No religion or philosophy can take a single decimal point away from the mathematical truism of sequential creation. Sunflowers, honey combs, pinecones, bacteria, the human face, the human body, and in fact the progression of molecular weights through the Periodic Table all obey this natural progression. The Golden Mean is the ratio by which chaos becomes order. Out of the quantum foam that makes up spacetime, and perhaps the consciousness soup that makes up dark matter and dark energy, order can arise without the addition of additional intelligent action by any outside influence. It might be called spontaneous generation, except that the mathematical relationship may actually be the intelligent influence from consciousness itself.

Someone asked me what the odds were that our universe turned out to be Carbon based. I told them one. That's right. You see, the only set of elements that can form is that supported by the mathematical ratio of the Golden Mean. Anything in between, or outside that ratio, cannot be supported by the universe. Therefore, all universes are Carbon based.

But we cannot always start at zero. Fibonacci had the right process, but the understanding of what could be realized with this process has nothing to do with the number zero.

Do we have to go all the way back to the beginning to find these ratios? No. Here is the breakthrough discovery that changed everything for me and opens the curtain of creation for each of you.

Any two numbers can be utilized in a Fibonacci Process, which we will now call the Phoenix Sequence as the power of this creative ratio rises out of the chaos of numbers. Now you can trust me on this, or you can try it yourself. I entered fractions, irrational numbers, and imaginary numbers, and the Phoenix Sequence worked every time. The most remarkable discovery was that even if quanta of energy were added together, the result was the same. This truly was the key to making manifestation, intention, and the Law of Attraction work by design.

Let's take any two numbers like 75 and 216. These two numbers are far apart. One is odd and one is even. They are not factors of one another. Yet, if we add the two numbers together, and then continue in a Fibonacci pattern for eight more iterations, the result will be the Golden Mean.   This is called the Phoenix Sequence. Amazed? Watch.

$$75 + 216 = 291$$
$$216 + 291 = 507$$
$$291 + 507 = 798$$
$$507 + 798 = 1305$$
$$798 + 1305 = 2103$$
$$1305 + 2103 = 3408$$
$$2103 + 3408 = 5511$$
$$3408 + 5511 = 8919$$

Now observe this: $\dfrac{8919}{5511} = 1.618$ This is the Golden Mean!

This is Phi (Φ), the original value realized when Source took the square root of itself to become each of you.   Awesome.   And, it will work with any two numbers, whether they are whole numbers or not with very little deviation from the plotted line.   The slope is always the Golden Mean, plus or minus a very small deviation.

We will show you this means that any starting point is suitable. "Now," would be excellent.   Add to this point the energy of a dream, as we will show you later in the book.   Like striking a bell with a hammer, the ring will go out into the universe and whatever will constructively resonate with that sound always in the Golden Ratio. The sound that returns to you will be the sound given off by that which resonated with the ring.

In other words, the starting point plus the ring produced a third energy; the first wave of resonance. When that wave arrives, you must precisely and exactly add another dose of energy. It can be in the form of work, a phone call, an email, or other type of action. Hence you have added the next iteration of energy to the dream. Doing so with the right thing and the right intensity is the key to success. The ability to listen to that return of the wave so that the exact timing of the next energy input can be achieved is the key to making dreams come true. It is the key to abundance.

The power behind this discovery is that two seemingly unrelated life experiences can be arranged into a string of events that fit the ratio by which the universe expands in order. *The Secret* is unlocked with this process followed for eight iterations or steps.

I interviewed three professional golfers for this book. I asked them how many times they tried to get on the pro tour before they were successful. Eight. I asked an investor how many times he invested in various companies before he made a large return on his investment. Eight. I asked real estate agents how many closings they had before they really got the swing of it and started making money consistently, almost as though it took half the effort to get the same results. Eight. In fact, consistent with the Phoenix Sequence, I discovered that every failure I interviewed only attempted to accomplish their dream two or three times before quitting.

We have shown you that if you go back to the past and add any two events on your path, no matter how distant in time, within eight additive motions the Golden Mean can be achieved. They must, however, be sequential. This means one event must be the driver or the opportunity to the next event. When a door closes, a window opens. You have to be able to listen and hear when the window opens and have the determination to jump through it when it does. This is equally functional with future movements. This is the process of perfect creation. Rotating the MerKaBa fields in ratios of the Golden Mean, with the female rotation as the higher of the two numbers, will produce the perfect manifestation field for human beings. The reason the MerKaBa is important is to help your Life Energy to flow and stay focused. The place to focus your energy is your heart. I'll explain more on this a little further in the book.

The Dream Process

Most people have dreams. If you don't have one, it is probably because you forgot the one you had when you were a child. We often make plans to accomplish the dream, but most of the time it does not manifest. The Phoenix Sequence does not need to start at zero. It can start anywhere. And, as we have now proven, once you start adding events to the sequence, within eight iterations, the process is obeying the Golden Mean, most likely in harmony with the universe.

Most people don't achieve their dreams because the door closes in front of them. If it is a good dream, another door often opens, and sometimes people keep walking for about three more doors. Then they quit. The universe will resonate with your intention, no matter what. But, if you quit before eight iterations, you will not succeed because the Golden Mean has not been realized. Does this mean you must experience seven failures before you experience a success? Possibly, but not likely. The joy you will feel because you are walking your dream process will be so great that you will already feel successful. In fact, finishing isn't the goal of a proper dream anyway. Dreams should be all about *doing* and *being*, rather than *having*. I am always amazed at how many people dream of having things rather than being something or processing something.

Many times when I ask people about their dream, they say they want a million dollars. Pressing further, I ask *why* they want the million dollars. They usually say something like they want to travel or be able to help others with their money. So, the real dream is not the money. Not really. It is usually the things the money can buy, or the fun that can be had spending it that is the real dream. Still, it is usually shallow and never brings joy.

We realize that dream building on *things* only gets us to a place where we are ready to die. In other words, when you get that red sports car you are dreaming about, is your life complete? Are you ready to die? Getting things or having things is a result of being and doing.

Being is the process I am trying to accomplish with sending this book back to you with all the knowledge of the ancients tied together with the learning of the End Times. **Being** is the <u>perfect present state</u> of an individual consciousness.

I feel that with the access to knowledge that you have in your time and the addition of the messages left by the ancients—though some may be veiled in symbols designed to convey the truth without costing them their lives—you would have all the tools you need to manifest proper and useful dreams. Dreams of *being* will naturally lead to the action of *doing*.

Doing is the actual energy applied to complete the state of BEING. When we bring our dream of being into the world of work in the three-dimensional world, the doing begins. This doing is the value of a mortal life. It is the true reason why we come to this dimension to do work. And, contrary to many teachings, this Earth is one of the best places in the universe to have a mortal life. Look at who has come here to experience a mortal life. Adam, Gandhi, Moses, and even Jesus came here to experience a mortal life. Don't feel like this is such a bad place.

The truth is that when someone asks you where heaven is, you need only say, "Right here." By the same token, when someone asks you where hell is, you need only say, "Right here." What I am trying to teach you is that you and only you can make this world a heaven or a hell. It can happen within the walls of your own home, or even within the walls of your own cells. As I mentioned earlier, the difference between an optimist and a pessimist is that the optimist believes we live in the best of all possible worlds, while the pessimist fears that's true. Same world...different realities.

So, before you finish this book you should know that dreaming is about *process* and not about *solids*. Working toward your dream is the goal. That is to say, serving as a schoolteacher is a good dream, because it is about the process of teaching. Dreaming of a red sports car is not a good dream because it is focusing on a solid that acts just like the sandcastle, ready to be jumped upon or washed away in the sea.

Fig. 20. The things of this world are distractions from our true nature as spiritual beings. (Photo by Author)

The thing to remember is to dream. As a child you had them. As a rational grownup you have been indoctrinated to believe in three-dimensional treasures as the goals of life. Be like the child again and dream of the sand castle.

Fig 21. Building the sand castle.

Like the child building the sand castle, the *process* of forming the castle with one's hands is the goal, not finishing the castle. Owning a fine home or having a million dollars in the bank is not a proper dream. Being a teacher or an engineer are suitable process-type dreams. The main idea to remember here is don't quit after two or three failures. Remember that the universe will flow things to you according to your intentions and your response to that flow must reach eight iterations before the Golden Mean can be realized.

Notice that there exists a pathway around the circumference of each of these photon-thin filaments. Keep in mind that a photon is considered a massless particle. We are only displaying the particle here so you can better imagine it with your three-dimensional brain. Just because it is massless, does not mean it does not exist. If you want to

157

see if they exist for yourself, just turn on a flashlight and observe the light beam. For a simple understanding, let's assume an irreducible complexity here. This light is formed by the photons generated when electrons move from one energy state to another around a molecule. Electrical current provided by the battery excites the electrons to a higher state. When the electrons jump between energy states, a photon at a frequency exactly matching that difference radiates out from that molecule. All frequencies in the visible and non-visible range obey this principle.

So, when we say that a photon moves through time, it forms a thread through the time cone that becomes part of the fabric. As human beings, we can and do emit billions of these photons each and every moment. When these photons move through space and time, they exhibit the properties of a wave. When we stop to see their spin, they behave as particles. This Wave-Particle duality has been the bane of physics for more than a century. Each photon has a spin that is either positive or negative. For our purposes, we want you to think of it as clockwise or counterclockwise. The spin of this particle can be reversed electromagnetically. This can either be done with sophisticated instruments or with human intention.

Recall the entangled particles we discussed earlier. These particles are created by an individual. They might be entangled with other human beings or even with beings that are not human. That means that when the spin is altered by you, the particle in the other being's time cone changes spin instantaneously. If the spin on the distant particle is altered by an energy in that environment, the spin of the matching particle in your time cone changes as well. Without any effort of your own, the energy condition has moved. An event or an act in your past can change through the intention of another being. You can change the past of another being by your intention as well. This is conditional upon the two particles being entangled. This normally means that the two of you had some kind of relationship or shared experience.

The limits on this activity are infinite. That is to say, the past can be, and is, constantly improved and altered by the intention of the participants. In physics, giant gravitons in large numbers as dielectric gravitational waves form fuzzy cylinders that mathematically behave in exactly the same manner.

Each thread is actually a pathway formed by the passing of the particle through time. Now, we can get a picture of how complex the relationships between a human being and the universe of other sentient beings can be. Even more clearly, we can see the effect of intention upon the universe. So let us do this with purpose.

Oh butterfly,
Distant flower desired,
Supped life's nectar
Without a single
Linear stroke
Of her painted wings.

Chapter 7: Manifestation of the Future

In this chapter, you're going to learn how to make *The Secret* work for you. In noise of the third dimensional world, like midtown Manhattan at 5:30 PM, is loud and chaotic at times. You are going to learn how to listen to the universe, so you will know when to move, when to exert the force of your intention, when to make the call, and when to tap that immoveable object. I know you don't believe that it will move with such a tiny amount of force, but believe me when I tell you this. The right amount of energy applied at exactly the right moment in the Golden Mean at least eight times in succession will move anything; even a mountain. I have watched three-inch steel tubing whip like a soft spaghetti noodle with only five pounds of weight vibrating at precisely the right frequency in the center. A two hundred pound man could jump all day and not make that bean move one inch, but a tiny little piston pressing down at the right frequency will produce vibrations with amplitude of more than 12 inches.

First, you are going to be taught how and where to go in order to pick up these timing signals from the universe. Then, you will be taught how to exert your force upon the universe at the right time for the maximum effect. You will be in the *zone* where the abundance of the universe will overflow your cup with more than you can enjoy.

You may have to share what you find there.

The intention of a sentient being is the most powerful force in the universe. It is the creative force of all things. Time itself is the creation of sentience. The singularity that is the universe has no such thing as time. Sentient beings who are sovereign have realized that mortality is one of the finest methods by which awareness can be realized. Taste bud by taste bud, the biological transducer we call the human body has been designed and extensively engineered to savor every morsel of existence.

A transducer is an instrument that converts inputs in one form to a common format for the operating system. For instance, extremely small differences in the amount of sodium chloride (table salt) can be differentiated through the chemical detectors located in the middle of the tongue. Color, in fact blends of colors, can be detected by the human eye. Both of these inputs are translated into electrical signals that are interpreted by the operating system of a super-computer called the human brain. In 2013, the first computer was invented that could match the average human brain for computing power.

In 2015, Irish scientists cracked the code for the human brain operating system and quaternary language was born and revealed to the world. The human brain is a lens through which the mind can view mortality. Boron coated silicon chips utilizing binary language had reached the clock speed limit and were replaced with nano-tech crystals capable of four switch states.

The debate still rages over whether the ions used in the crystals for switches, called BITs (Beryllium Ion Terminals), were actually individual particles and not the same bilocating particle. Computer security concerns were well founded. Clock speeds of BIT processors could not be measured, as information seemed to process before it was even entered into the computer. Information collisions were described in the July, 2016 issue of Wired Magazine as being like tossing a baseball through a wormhole and having it return before you threw it. I know it sounds impossible, but those of you reading this book in the past will just have to wait and see that it is, in fact, true.

Human beings have ego that, unlike the butterfly we talked about earlier, tries to draw a straight line between the present and the future. As I have already shown you, these straight lines are called future threads. They lack dimension and quality and vastly attenuate the amount of energy the universe can bring back to you from distant times. Learning to allow the universe and your *life force* to flow together is the antithesis of three-dimensions, but it will feel quite natural when you are out of your body and into your heart.

This chapter is vital for the future of the human race on Earth, and thus the entire galaxy, for you to learn how to manifest the future. The future unfolds like a world with no horizon and not according to any teleological design. That is to say, there is no preset pattern by which the lives of humans unfold like a cosmologically digital recording. As in the movie *Bedazzled*, Elizabeth Hurley's devilish character granted wishes, but always withheld some vital part of the gift so at to bring misery to Brandon Fraser.

You have been handed the keys to the future and it will be

chosen by you as you see fit. Time is merely the rate at which we seem to behold the universe. In fact, the truth is that nothing—absolutely nothing—is fixed in the universe.

Fig. 22. Cartoon illustrating that our ability to choose success is empowered by our knowledge of the future.

But human beings have the ability to comprehend alternate time lines. We are by spiritual nature not bound to three-dimensional time. It is only our mortal bodies that are locked into the linear flow of time. This is the reason minutes turn into hours, and days or even months turn into a few minutes when we consider them. When we're on vacation, the days go by like seconds. When we're at work, the last few minutes of the day can take hours.

The only manageable segment of time is the moment. This is a snapshot of distance that can be considered by a human being. The culture of the Earth in the year 2010 was built around planning for the future of retirement and leisure. Those who could contribute to their 401-K account retired on the golf course with new cars in the garage. Those who did not plan for the future, retired in poverty on Social Security. Turning over one's sovereignty to the government is one of the main causes of destruction of the ability to manifest one's future.

The responsibility for the life condition was abdicated through deception. People ended up working lives they hated for thirty or forty years so they could retire in comfort. But they usually were in such poor health and had long since lost sight of their dream by the time they retired that they could not have joy. They forced a future thread through the cone of time and passed by the bounty the universe displayed all around them every microsecond of every day.

This chapter will help you learn to listen for the bounty of the universe around you. It will teach you a method of preventing yourself from forcing a future thread through the cone of time. Instead, like the butterfly, you will fix your sight on the dream of the flower, and then beat your wings with proper timing, but no preconception of a particular path to the flower. The universe will not only support your wings—notwithstanding some turbulence for variety and experience— but will provide you rich supply all the days of your existence.

The most important thing is that you will always be on your purpose, without sacrifice and without letting the sun go down without gratitude for every experience in your life. The variety and wonder of life will fill volumes of your journals. And the dream of retirement will drift away, because you will never want to stop what you are doing. Like the Buddha described, once you place your foot onto the path you are already at your destination. True motorcycle enthusiasts don't ride to get to a certain place. Simply letting out the clutch with the engine running *is* the destination.

The greatest challenge in mortal life is to define one's dream. "What do I want to be when I grow up?" is the hardest question in the universe to answer. This involves a healthy exercise. We must look far into the future without much information to go on. When we are young, it is particularly difficult. Or is it? We emulate positions like astronauts or firefighters when we're little boys; or actresses and flight attendants when we're little girls. What do you think it would be like to be able to stop any moment of any day and say, "I am doing what I always wanted to do?"

This is known as being *on purpose*. In the cone of time, there is always a finite number of choices we can make every microsecond. The curse perpetuated by religionists that we can never be perfect is wrong. Period. Perfection is merely a stage of completion. We can be and are perfect all the time. You are the perfect individual receiving the sum total karma of your choices from all of your existences. Nothing but this result can occur. It is perfect and you are perfect, *just as your father who is in heaven is perfect.*

So, when we look at the dream flower, the nature of humans is to imagine being at the flower. Then we draw a step back, and then another, and then another until we are standing at the present moment in time. This is called the *but first list*. "I want to accomplish this," we say to ourselves, "but first I must do this, and then I must do this, etc."

Our training tells us that if we follow that path of but-first bread crumbs from the future, we will have no choice but to arrive at the flower. Ta dah. Retirement. This is the great deceptive marketing plan of mortal life, because we have drawn our own future thread to the goal, and the universe most likely holds no resonant support for that thread, therefore the goal is *prevented* from being supported by the

165

very intention you placed into the universe. Therefore, you are reaping only a fraction of the fulfillment you dreamt about.

Ah ha! So the flower is not the dream after all. Like the sand castle we mentioned in Figure 22, the process can be creative and artistic and can involve hours or days. Then, it is finished. What do you do then? Walk away. Jump on it. Wait for the tide to come in a wash it away.

The point is that the sand castle is not the goal. It is the building of the sand castle that is the goal. The joy comes from the building, not from the completion. The purpose of building was the dream. When you are on purpose, there is no need to finish the sand castle, unless it happens to be a precursor to the larger dream. The action of building while focused on the sand castle is the true dream.

Now, what we have done holographically is to explain to you that we can move through time while focused on a target without drawing a future thread. The whole image is already there, but the resolution and rich details are filled in with more and more effort until it becomes solid in this third dimensional reality. A future thread is the "but first" list that we might create when we consider a task or goal. The corporate world and the *on purpose* world are compatible, believe it or not. The idea is to encapsulate or compartmentalize the worlds inside one another.

So, let's consider resonance from the universe. Remember the example of the sympathetic resonance using the guitar leaning against the wall? What we want to share with you is the ability to present your guitar to the universe so you can resonate with the bounty that is there for you. For now, we'll teach you about this in *receive mode*. Then we'll teach you about the *send mode*.

With the understanding that there have been many thousands of books written on this subject by the year 2010, we seek not to compare this discovery to any of those penned by myriads of self-help gurus. This is the discovery of the use of intention to manifest the future. It is designed to work with the purpose of your heart. Although this training may not fill your bank account with millions of dollars, unless that is the path of resonance the universe will support for you, it will fill your life with the flow of joy that you imagined the money would bring you.

You may have thought the million dollars would give security while not having to work a full-time job, the opportunity to meet really neat people, and to travel the world. But if you could travel the world, meet all kinds of really neat people, and have security without the million dollars, you have still reached your goal. Haven't you? So why would you force the universe to give you a million dollars when that may not be the method by which your true objectives can be met?

How and Where to Listen

So, here we go. Step by step, this is how and where to listen to the future. Masters trained and vetted over thousands of years have developed this method, but this is the first time it has ever been applied to resonance theory. You are about to learn how to listen to the energy you started with your dream intention. It has a particular feeling to it that you cannot recognize if you are wrapped up in your three dimensional world. It's too noisy here. If you miss the signal, you won't know when to apply your energy, like the phone call to the job prospect, or the presentation to the investor, or the conversation with the lover of your dreams.

The place is in your heart. So, along with the master teachers from whom I have benefitted, we will show how to get there and do some looking around.

Step One – Getting in the heart.

The goal of the first step is to reach the heart. Being *in the heart* allows us to be aware of the universe and to tune our intention to the universe. Here is how that is done in writing. This usually takes more practice for men that it does women, but it can be achieved by everyone.

The heart is a very unique organ, to be sure. But most people don't know that it actually contains some gray matter. That's right. The heart contains brain cells. This is a section of the heart that if harmed during surgery it may never be the same, and the patient may even die.

The more remarkable realization is that human beings may actually have the ability to *think* with their hearts. Not all contemplation is done in the frontal lobe of the brain in the cerebral cortex. Neurological research has shown that even humans missing their cerebral cortex, and in fact most of their brains, can still think and wonder and function with genius.

168

The hypothalamus and pineal glands are the subjects of volumes of speculation, but in pure thought, it is the heart where the singularity is accessed. The heart is the launching pad for your consciousness. You recall my launching patio on the red Sun planet? You're going to find your place as well. So get ready. There is some preparation for getting in the heart.

The MerKaBa meditation is the most efficient method I have seen for enabling a person to reach his or her heart. I run three companies and have no time to waste sitting around in twisted shapes trying to reach an empty state of mind. The MerKaBa is seventeen breaths and takes less than 8 minutes to accomplish. With practice the person may imagine being in the heart without going through the MerKaBa meditation, but I highly recommend that you try the MerKaBa meditation – also called the Flower of Life meditation – for at least six months before you decide to stop doing it.[12] As soon as you quit, in fact a soon as you think about stopping, you will feel a difference in how you receive knowledge. The energy field generated by the MerKaBa meditation may last as long as forty-eight hours, but daily meditation is far more successful at enabling this process. Here is how it works.

There are seventeen conscious breaths to reach this point. Using the audio CD *MerKaBa II* recorded by Maureen St. Germain[13] is the best way to master the timing. A point of fact you might enjoy. Whales only breathe consciously. They have been witnessed by Joan

---

[12] http://www.floweroflife.org
[13] http://www.maureenstgermain.com

Ocean holding states of meditation that we can only dream about. You can find the CD just by searching for the *MerKaBa II* recorded by Maureen St. Germain. There are some points that are critical that we will discuss in detail below.

The Breaths and Mudras

The following numbered items are individual breaths in a sequence designed to prepare a physical body for conscious contact with the higher self, or source. This includes finger and hand positions called mudras. These connect energy body circuits for the body and facilitate the flow of Life Force.

1. Touch the tip of the index finger of each hand to the tip of the thumb forming a ring, close your eyes and inhale through your nose fully.

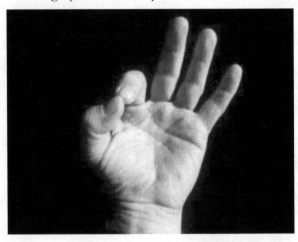

Fig. 23. Mudra with thumb and index finger.

While doing this, imagine the sky tetrahedron around your body filled with light. You're not filling it with light. It is already filled with light, marked by the solid lines at the edges of the tetrahedron as if they were strings pulled tight.

Fig. 24. Star Tetrahedron. The Tetrahedron pointing up is the Sky Tetrahedron, and the one pointing down is the Earth Tetrahedron. The MerKaBa Field extends with a 27.5 foot radius on the plane of the arrows.

Keep your throat open as though you were about to blow out a candle. It takes about three seconds to visualize the tetrahedron shape. For men, the edge of the tetrahedron faces forward parallel to the bridge of the nose. For women, the flat face of the tetrahedron faces forward parallel with the bridge of the nose. Exhale through the nose all the way until the lungs are empty. Close the throat, not allowing any air to enter the lungs. Imagine the Earth tetrahedron filled with light. Observe that there are impurities like clumps of negativity in your life coalescing inside that tetrahedron. Open the eyes, slightly cross the eyes, and sweep them up and down, then close them again. This process is called the *Pulse*. It is widely accepted that the eyes are the main avenue for light to enter the body. In this respect they are also like lasers pointing out to the universe. In this exercise, we are crossing the laser beams to form a wiper of sorts, to clean away the negative energy that coalesces in the Earth tetrahedron. If you try it, you will see that it works, and it keeps you from dropping through the hypnagogia into sleep. It is designed to sweep the negativity out of the light. As soon as this is done, continue to breath 2.

2. Move the thumb of each hand to the second finger and repeat the breathing cycle.

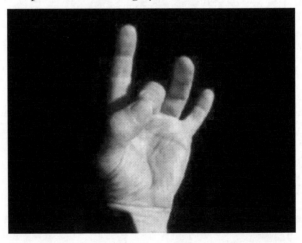

Fig. 25. Mudra with thumb and second finger.

3. Move the thumb of each hand to the ring finger and

repeat the breathing cycle and the Pulse.

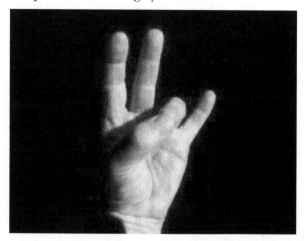

Fig. 26. Mudra with thumb and ring finger.

4.   Move the thumb of each hand to the little finger and repeat the breathing cycle and the Pulse.

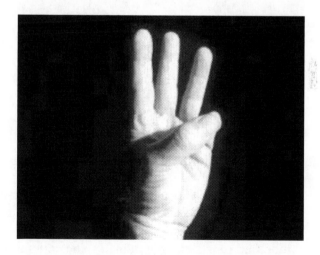

Fig. 27. Mudra with thumb and little finger.

5.   Move the thumb of each hand back to the index finger and repeat the breathing cycle and the Pulse.

6.   Move the thumb of each hand to the second finger and repeat the breathing cycle and the Pulse.

7.   Move the thumb of each hand so that it touches the index finger and the second finger. While keeping the eyes shut, imagine a small laser pointer pinched between this finger union. Aim that imaginary light beam, like you are holding a laser pointer, coming from the spot where the fingers and thumb meet directly at your third eye in the forehead. Repeat the process of breathing and the Pulse one last time.

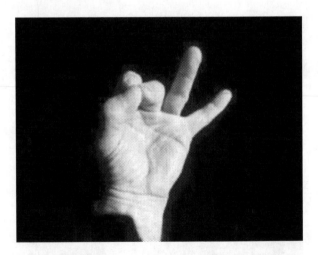

Fig. 28. Mudra with thumb and index and second fingers.

8.   Keep the same finger position, except we are no longer clearing the negativity from the Earth tetrahedron. Now we want you imagine the Prana (life sustaining Force) tube that runs along the human spine with an opening at the top and bottom. The tube is open to the sky and the Earth. We want you to imagine drawing energy into your body through this tube from both directions. This energy will collect in your body just behind the belly button. With this breath, it will form a light crystal the size of a

baseball.

9.   Keep the same finger position. Remember to breathe deeply and exhale completely and consciously. The spirit is beginning to expand away from the physical body, so concentration is required here or you will drift away and forget to breathe correctly. Keep gathering energy through the Prana tube. The ball of light is the size of a basketball. It is gaining light and is the color of a harvest moon.

10.   Keep the same finger position. When the breath is completely taken in, hold the breath slightly, building pressure. The ball of light is now the color of the sun and very bright. With great intention and power, force the breath out like you're trying to blow out a candle five feet away. Imagine the ball of light instantly blowing up to a diameter of about six feet, with the small, round crystal light in the center. They are bright and spinning. The direction is not important at this time, only that they are not spinning at the same rate, or that the smaller crystal is barely revolving, and the larger sphere is revolving at high speed. They are not stable yet. You may have a sensation of wobbling while you are sitting. In fact, someone observing you in this state of meditation will notice a slight wobble if you're in the seated position.

11.   Keep the same finger position. Real concentration is required here, so you don't drift away too soon. This breath is deep and conscious, in and out through the nose, using the same amount of time for both. During this breath the stability of the spheres is the goal. Try to synchronize the revolutions so the spheres do not wobble. The spheres are concentric. That is to say, they are exactly surrounding one another. All you have to imagine is the crystal spheres stabilizing. They will do this naturally, but there will be a very strong temptation

175

to drift into sleep.

12. Keep the same finger position and use the same breathing technique. Maintain your concentration, as it does take three full breaths for this process to complete. During this breath the stability of the spheres is the goal. Try to synchronize the revolutions so the spheres do not wobble.

13. Keep the same finger position. The breath is still deep and conscious. During this breath the stability of the spheres is the goal. Try to synchronize the revolutions so the spheres do not wobble.

14. Now, imagine moving the center of the spheres from the belly to your heart. Imagine moving the stable and bright spheres to center on your heart, just left of the center of your chest. Change the hand positions so that the hands are flattened. The male will rest the back of his left hand in the palm of his right hand, with the first knuckle in behind the first knuckle of the other hand (see Figure 30). Females will rest their hands in the opposite configuration (See Figure 31). Extend the thumbs and touch them, forming a triangle in front of the hands pointing away from the body. The breaths become shallow here. Stay here as long as you like, but we must keep moving along. Tell yourself that you want to be in your heart. Imagine traveling from the Pineal Gland, just above the roof of the mouth, down the trachea to a point just to the right of your heart. Consciously, move to the left, through the muscle and directly into your heart. You will notice a void there. It should feel like a point between two vortexes. Consciously, in your mind, say the words, "Let there be light."

Fig. 29. Mudra with hands nested (male).

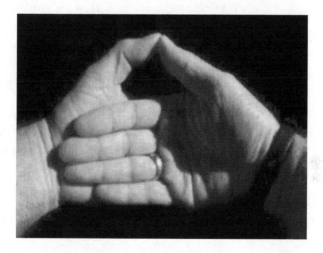

Fig. 30. Mudra with hands nested (female).

15. Your hands will remain in this mudra position for the rest of the meditation. Take a deep breath in through the nose, but do not close the throat. Imagine the other two star tetrahedron fields that are not fixed. One is going to start rotating to the counterclockwise or female direction, the other is going to rotate in the clockwise or male direction. Just get them spinning. These are complete star tetrahedrons, and not the individual tetrahedrons (sky

177

and Earth). The sky and Earth tetrahedrons are locked together as a set. Exhale with a forced breath as before. This act is like using the force of your intended breath to make the star tetrahedrons spin the way you want them to spin.

16.   Inhale completely and bring the two star tetrahedrons to 9/10 the speed of light in a ratio of thirty-four to the left, and twenty-one to the right. This is the Fibonacci sequence of increase. Note that 34 divided by 21 is 1.619, which is very close to Phi 1.618. This ratio is the resonant ratio of increase known as the Golden Mean. All you have to do is say to yourself, "Thirty-four to the left and twenty-one to the right," and it will be so. Exhale with a forced breath as though you are trying to blow out a candle a few feet away.

17.   Inhale completely through the nose and spin the star tetrahedrons at the speed of light with that ratio in mind. You don't have to over-think this. They will assume that ratio if you command them to do so. Exhale with a forced breath as before. Your MerKaBa is now set in motion and will remain in place for forty-eight hours.

Continue to meditate as long as you need from here with your breathing more shallow and regular. Your MerKaBa is now activated.

Step Two – Learning to intend with intention

Now that your MerKaBa has been activated, and you know how to get into your own heart, we can work on sending and receiving from the higher being within you. The human body is a very capable electromagnetic transmitter and receiver. The cell membranes of your body actually function like a liquid crystal, changing state with stimuli,

178

just like a computer, but with the power of an interdimensional transceiver. Your body is also capable of receiving energy from multiple dimensions, especially through the heart area. It is an even more prolific transmitter, whether you are aware of it or not. It can send energy across the universe, as the singularity contains no distance at all, instantaneously.

The intention of a human being is sent out whether it is intended or not. Lest that not make sense, we want to clarify. You will send out positive of negative energy at all times, even after death. You can send out this energy reflexively, just like the knee struck with the rubber mallet, or you can change the form and frequency of that energy with your intention. You can be acted upon by the energies in the universe, or you can act upon the universe. The choice is yours. You have almost all the tools. Here is the final tool you need to take conscious control of this subconscious process. Using these breaths and this process, you will be able to change the course of your life, your family, your community, and the planet. Our hope is that enough of you can be enabled and trained so that the average reality of the universe is shifted away from the conditions we inherited from you in the year 2015.

The Eighteenth Breath – the Key to Manifestation

This realm of concentration will become your most powerful and peaceful place for manifestation and reflection. The state of body that works best is the one between sleep and wakefulness. It takes a little practice to master this, but it won't take forty years in a Tibetan monastery to get great results. Most of the MerKaBa meditation instructors talk about the eighteenth breath, but they do not teach it. It is an individual thing. However there are some common attributes to this meditation, while you are in the heart that I can impart to you. They work. They are extremely useful in helping you conquer the three-dimensional hold on your spirit. Here we go.

The eighteenth breath can be done anytime you need to concentrate, but we recommend it *after* you have completed the first seventeen breaths and activated your MerKaBa tetrahedrons to the speed of light in the 21:34 ratio.

Use caution when initiating this form of breathing. Do not drive or operate equipment while breathing in this manner. Do not do this while lying in the hot tub, as you may run the risk of drowning. Using this breathing technique will disconnect your spirit from your body and may initiate an Out of Body Experience (OBE) within minutes. You may experience a buzzing sound or a sudden phase shift that feels awkward at first. It will place you into a controlled state of hypnagogia.[14] It is highly likely that you will experience an OBE if you perform this properly.

Precise timing of the breaths is the key to stabilizing the field we want you to create, although the depth of the breath can be adjusted to avoid hyperventilation or hypoventilation. Try to get as

---

[14] hypnagogia, in one or both senses, includes 'presomnal' or 'anthypnic sensations', 'visions of half-sleep', 'oneirogogic images' and 'phantasmata' 'the borderland of sleep', 'praedormitium', the 'borderland state', 'half-dream state', 'pre-dream condition, 'sleep onset dreams', dreamlets, and 'wakefulness-sleep transition' state

close to three seconds for each step changes as possible. The closer you get to three seconds for each breathing action, the more effective your energy transfer will become to and from the universe, because the magnetic field you are creating under the Pineal Gland will be tuned to the right level. In fact, the Pineal Gland will become trained to trigger DMT and Serotonins within minutes of starting to breathe in this manner, so make sure you are not in a position to fall down and hurt yourself. If you do this lying down, you will most likely fall asleep. I recommend a chair or a large floor pillow to sit on in a comfortable position. Crossing the legs might be comfortable for some and help support the hands in nested position, but sitting in a chair with a pillow in your lap to support your hands will work just fine.

While your hands are in the mudra assumed at the fourteenth breath, with the hands nested and the thumbs touching, I want you to change your breathing pattern. Remember, the energy body of humans for males is different than that of females. The body tetrahedrons are oriented differently, and the mudras are different. The male cups his left hand face up in his right hand, and the female cups her right hand face up in her left hand.

This is a twelve-second cycle, made of four three-second breathing actions. It is easy to do, but to do it perfectly over a period of time like 15 minutes will take practice. Balancing in hypnagogia is a little like trying to ride a unicycle. Some make it look easy, but it does take practice. Follow this procedure:

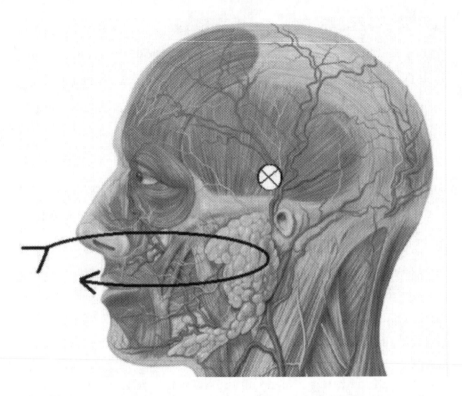

Fig. 31. The "X" is the location for the Pineal Gland. The arrowed path is the motion of the air of each breath. (image courtesy of WikiCommons; Patrick J. Lynch, medical illustrator and C. Carl Jaffe, MD, cardiologist.)

Method for the Eighteenth Breath

Place the tongue lightly against the roof of the mouth. This does two things. First, it completes a circuit between the tongue and the 6th Chakra behind the eyes. Second, it will act like a one-way valve for the air flow that requires very little effort.

When inhaling, let the air come in through the nose. When exhaling, let the air out through the mouth. This one-way movement of air establishes an electrical field just below the Pineal Gland, shown in Figure 31. This is a 12-second cycle. The timing is important, even though the size of the actual breath may vary to meet your needs for oxygen. As the need subsides, and you relax even further, the breathing will be shallow, but maintain the timing. This act of control is called Conscious Breathing.

Timing the breaths can be tricky, so I utilize my index finger against the back of my hand that is in the mudra from the 14th breath shown above in Figure 29 or Figure 30, depending if you're male or female. Tap the finger gently against the hand to make the timing easier.

1. Take a three-second breath through the nose. The depth of this breath will vary, depending on your blood-oxygen content. That is to say, some people will need to start with deep breaths to feel like they're getting enough air. As you progress into the depths of this meditation, the breaths will naturally become very shallow for the three seconds.

2. Hold this breath at the peak of the inhale for three seconds while keeping your throat open. It is like preparing to blow a candle out, but you do not inhale or exhale. Hold the inhale for three seconds only.

3. Exhale for three seconds through the mouth. Make the breath even all the way through. Try not to blow out quickly and then taper off the breath. Make it smooth and even all the way to the end, taking the full three seconds to exhale. Keep the lips slightly parted and use the tongue against the roof of the mouth like a sort of one-way valve. This will accomplish two things. First, it takes no effort or thought to control the way you inhale or exhale. Second, it connects the tongue to the Chakra behind the eyes. Many masters have told us that this circuit connection is important for the energy vortex to form beneath the pineal gland properly.

4. Hold the exhalation with the lungs completely empty for three seconds while keeping the throat open. Do not close the throat. It is as though you are about to take a breath, but

you hold yourself at the peak of emptiness instead. This is a very low-energy physical state and can be mastered to operate while you are nearly unconscious. This is known as the *release*. It is the most powerful action for setting the pure thought adrift in the vacuum of space. It is also where most people report hearing the buzzing sound or the pulse of energy coming back from the universe. It is the place of epiphany. It is when you are most quiet, and thus able to receive the minutest truth from the universe. This ends the twelve-second cycle. Repeat this for as long as you feel necessary.

There is an amazing physical transformation you will realize in just a few breaths. Your physical body begins to separate from your spirit body. You will feel the disconnection almost immediately and with a little practice you may be able to easily travel to distant places and times. It will take some discipline to control the wandering, because you have some work to do here. The objective is not to empty the mind, but to find the energy that resonates with your intention. At first, it may feel like looking for a needle in a haystack, but with only a small amount of practice, you will be able to draw it to you.

Shepherds in ancient times used to drive their sheep into a high-walled canyon or dry river bed to protect them from wolves while the shepherd went to town to do business. One or two shepherds could guard many flocks of sheep on a sort of rotation shift. When the shepherd returned, he could simply call his sheep, and only his sheep would respond to his voice. Jesus used this very parable in teaching his followers saying, "My sheep hear my voice, and I know them, and they follow me."[15]

You really don't want to drift into sleep and lose control of your conscious breathing. I highly recommend learning to tap your fingers together lightly as a sort of metronome. Most people start out using their heartbeat as the rhythm, but the heartbeat very soon slows down so much that they lose the timing. I do not recommend using music as the metronome. This will distract you from the smaller energies you may sense from the universe. Most people will lose track of their breathing and revert to autonomic breathing, because they slip into moments of unconsciousness. Whole minutes may transpire without breathing, until the person crosses back into consciousness and realizes he has lost control of the breathing technique. That's alright. You will get better and better at this breathing cycle.

This conscious breathing technique will work, and it is easy to master. Let me stress again that whatever you do, never try this breathing technique while operating any equipment or driving a car. Your bodies will separate, and you will be able to freely move between them. You will be out of touch with your physical body for up to 15 minutes at a time, but even 1 second of inattention can result in an accident. Your blood pressure will drop, as will your heart rate, so make sure you can't fall out of a chair and hurt yourself.

This is a tremendous support for you just before going into a meeting, or to take an exam, or to begin studying a complex concept you must memorize. It is awesome for problem solving and handling

---

[15] King James Bible: John 10:27

difficult situations, because the ability to travel to the future and look back at the challenge you're about to face really makes it easier to handle. You can look back from the future and say, "Hey, that wasn't so bad." You know the old saying *hindsight is 20-20* ? Well, using this technique of breathing, you get to have the hindsight *before* event happens in the physical world. You get to select the optimum response for those challenges. You may even be able to break that cycle of anger you have being trying your whole life to stop. You may pick up on the optimum chance for a romantic gesture ahead of time. If anyone is critical of your new found practice, tell them to study theoretical physics.

Remember, whales do not breathe autonomically. They only breathe consciously. As I mentioned before, whales have been observed by marine biologists, such as Jonathan Stearn, to achieve deep states of meditation toning deeply with their heads pointing down toward the ocean floor. This sound level can reach 170 decibels, the intensity of a jet engine, while the whales are in these states of apparent meditation. The songs can be complex, last around 30 minutes, and are often repeated several times in a row. Immersed in the same water, the meditative tones vibrated through the human body at the same time. The experience is reportedly quite heavenly. You will experience this many times inside your heart while performing the eighteenth breath.

Your awareness will be heightened to areas of extreme sensitivity, even lucidity, during meditation using this breathing technique. Your placement in time will appear inconsequential, and thus your ability to alter the effects past events have had on your life, in the moment they actually occurred. In other words, you will actually be able to change the way you are affected in real time as though you were reliving the event again, this time with the knowledge you now possess from the future.

When a human being expresses himself with power, whether he intends it or not, that expression sends out a *karma wave* that is very similar to the photon of light we discussed earlier, instantly across the universe. It can freely pass through time forward or backward, as both directions are equally accessible to energy. Remember, when you access a period, it will be affected by your presence and observation.

Be mindful of the energy you take to these places. This technique can be used for good or ill, but generally, the effects are self correcting. Dark thoughts will not resonate with the universe very well, unless the sentient being chooses to exist in that area where those thoughts will resonate. Likewise, bliss and melancholy will also be self-correcting. Joy and gratitude are the best energies to perpetrate. It may sympathetically resonate with anyone or anything that is nearby or distant, present or past, that is receptive to that vibration.

This means that from an energetic point of view, human beings can be like a bull in a china shop. We can display nearly unlimited power in an environment that might contain very delicate and expensive things and people. Whether we intend to or not, we may crash around destroying everything in our path. We may throw a tantrum if things are not going our way, having unwittingly caused the very conditions that are upsetting the world. Reflecting energies perpetrated upon you will most assuredly set up repeating cycles of failure in your life. We may also offer mercy and gratitude to our enemies, which can influence their treatment of you or your concerns. This also adds no energy for resonation of the failure or defeat that seems to follow you when you do add energy and dwell upon those things. Talking about it, or repeating it to your friends or coworkers, will create a behemoth of failure that will follow you down the frozen food section at the grocery, and into the pew at church, and into your bed at night.

As we have discussed earlier, one hundred percent of your life is the result of your choices and your energy. As we have mentioned earlier, all matter and all beings are conscious. Most every being is simply not conscious that it is conscious.

Also as we have mentioned earlier, the feedback from the universe will come to you, based on your intention. You were not given the toolbox to be able to know when it is coming, and how many steps you must take to allow your action on the universe to resonate with you. Remember, it takes eight iterations, so don't give up after the first three failures.

Thousands of people we have interviewed have life books full of failure and disappointment from three-page track records. They send out their dream intention and then walk through only three or four doors before giving up. This is the most important thing to remember when manifesting the future.

When the universe sends a resonation event to you, you must act immediately. Swinging the bat a second too late doesn't do anything but stir up the dust. Remember the plates of metal that were drawn into place ahead of Magneto as he walked across the chasm in the movie *X-Men*? Remember playing the game of tetherball? Remember losing your job and thinking the world was coming to an end, only to find an even better job a few weeks later?

When a door closes, a window opens…but only for a moment. If you don't hear the window open because your mind was too noisy, or you stood there enjoying the view through the opening and didn't jump through, the resonation cycle may end. If you were standing out in the street looking up at the sky and cursing God, you will not hear the momentary opportunity open for you. You will lose the energy building from each tiny effort toward your dream.

As each karma wave yield arrives, you must be listening and ready to add your precisely measured energy to the wave so it will gain strength through constructive interference. Do so with calm and faith, because after all, you are the creator. You are god. You are lord. You and you alone are your judge. You cannot, and have never been, separated from Source. If you are aimless, or cursing God because you have not immediately received your desire in full, then you will not be capable of adding energy to the wave as it comes by. This lack of resonant energy from you almost always results in the wave dying out and never coming back.

When you reach the eighth iteration, you must be very careful to listen closely to the universe. Pay close attention to your energy output. If you are negative, cynical, or fearful, you will block the blessings coming to you from the resonance with your dream. If you force your own future threads into existence, then you block the universe from resonating with your dream much like a capo added to the neck of a guitar. All the pitches have changed, like flowers coming from rain and sunshine, and may sound nothing like the composition you imagined. The best place to do this listening is in your heart, while performing the eighteenth breath process.

When you are quiet, you can hear the universe. When the next step comes along, you will be perfectly fitted hear it, and you will be ready to step forward on it like a freshly formed stepping stone of glass. Through listening and synchronicity, you will move irreversibly toward your dream through the process of constructive interference. Even the best masters teach endurance. Every single sport is won in the last few moments. The team that walks away from the eighth inning, or the third quarter, or the penultimate play, loses. Remember this very carefully. <u>You are not competing against anyone except yourself</u>. You are trying to become what you want to be. You are trying to do what you want to do. For good or for ill, it will be so.

Above all, keep in mind that <u>it does not matter how much you are loved. It only matter how much you love others.</u> Praying for the destruction of your enemies only lowers your own frequency. This is a self-checking system. Building darkness and fear will not resonate with light, and will result in only darkness and fear.

Praying that the hearts of your enemies will be softened and that they will receive peace and become comfortable in the light will raise you up and send vibrations that only resonate with light. If the darkness is not constructively altered by the observation of that light, then it will dissolve like a single handclap on a deserted beach.

The entire universe, and all forms of life, is inside of you. You carry the DNA of all beings in the entire universe inside of you. Your body is made of matter that is inextricably entangled with the Earth, the universe, and with Source. If you feel further from God today than you did yesterday, who moved?

Cherish every leaf and every wave crashing on the shore. Not many planets have life or liquid water on their surface. Cherish every kiss and every time you give birth. Stare at your children when they are sleeping and never forget their skin and their eyelashes closed softly against their curious eyes.

Linger just a moment longer when you embrace someone or make love. See the being within the human. Know that this being is not from here either. Seek out your soul mates. All of them. If you cannot bring yourself to love them in this lifetime, then touch them and let them know you remember what you once had, and that it is among your most treasured memories, and that they will always live on it you. Gather at the best places on Earth and remember your last world and the things you always wanted to do.

If your quest for wealth is preventing you from doing those things or being what you want to be, you now know what to do. Wealth may very well not be the way the universe can deliver your objective to you. If you have manifested wealth as an objective, you have drawn a large future thread of your own for which there is no resonating energy in the universe.

Proper dreaming and goal setting are the most challenging of the skills you have to learn. Remember to let the bounty of the universe flow to you, and do not draw your own future threads to your dream. The dream will happen if you just let go of the air in your lungs and let the water flow through your fingers. It will return to you with the place for you to stand so the ball will fall in your glove.

The joy of your life will not be in houses, but rather in homes; even if they are borrowed and you must crash weddings with your children to have a decent meal with punch and ice cream for dessert. The treasures of mortality are not in money or gold, but in the bounty and mercy you offer others.

Afterword

Since the inception of this series of books in 2001, the efforts to send back Part Two from the year 2015, and after nearly six years of writing our results of more than fifty years of research, we have changed. Rather, I have evolved…along with you. Where once I may have been indoctrinated, I have reached much further into the maelstrom of knowledge from many worlds. I have gathered strength and testimony from direct contact with the most powerful love in the universe. I have come to know you and met thousands of people around the country as we have toured to speak and try to raise support for our projects.

Many people have asked me to tell the story of what happened during the 2006 ECETI Conference at Mount Adams in Washington. This may not be everything that happened, but it will give you an idea of how all this comes full circle and begins to make sense. On August 20th of 2006, I was asked to lecture about the first Volume of *The Ark of Millions of Years*. The preparation for the talk ended up changing the course of my life. Or should I say, it reawakened what had fallen asleep in me many decades ago. The first day of the event I had been reintroduced to meditation as a way to access information out there in the universe. I didn't expect anything to happen except to reacquaint myself with that state of relaxation I knew as a youth while practicing Transcendental Meditation.

The night before my lecture I had joined a small group with a clear view of Mount Adams in calm meditation. Within minutes we were all quiet deep into our respective meditative states. I cannot tell how much time passed before the event that would change my world for a second time transpired.

I began to feel a soft pulse against my heart area. At first, I thought it was my own heart beating. I did a quick and silent check of my own body only to discover that it was not my heart beating. It was coming from outside my body. It felt as though I was being rhythmically touched on the outside of my heart area with a soft pillow. I became aware of a conduit, as it were, open and connected to the mountain and directly to my heart. It was so interesting and felt so good, that I stayed with it. There was no sense of panic, no sense of alarm. I felt serene and unthreatened.

I very soon became aware of singing. It was like a choir with ten thousands voices in it. The harmonies were endless, layers upon layers of basses and sopranos and tenors and even other voices upon voices were continuing with this choir. I thought at this point that the event host, James Gilliland at the ECETI *ranch*, had turned on some music, but this was not the case. The sound was not coming through my ears. It was coming through my heart. It felt like it was resonating through the frame of my body. Three words came out of this amazing symphony of voices. *Peace* was the first word; and it was sustained for what seemed several minutes. *Love* was the next word, equally sustained and amazingly beautiful. *Joy* was the final word in the series, and then the series repeated. Over a period of what seemed half an hour—it could have been much longer—the series was laid into my heart from the mountain. The experience was like bathing in sound, with droplets of energy rinsing every care from my soul. Three long and soothing times this series of words were repeated.

As mysteriously as it began, this heavenly chorus faded into silence. The conduit remained connected to my heart as the continuous echoes subsided like the last few birds in a white flock of birds with musical feathers flew away down the conduit back to the mountain. As the silence became quiet there was a voice that came. It was clean and clear. The words were something I never expected to hear in this life.

"Because you are quick to forgive, you are forgiven." The effect was stunning. Just as the tears of joy were about to burst upon my meditative calm, the conduit suddenly disconnected. The sound inside my body was like a giant pressure hose being disconnected from my heart. Decompressing with a rushing sound, my body recoiled as though I had been holding onto this conduit with all my might when it popped loose from my chest. I gasped for air and grabbed for something to prevent myself from falling over backwards against the floor behind me.

Friends were there to catch me. One of my closest and dearest friends had been watching me, because something had caught her attention as well during this event. "Did you see that?" I asked with a shudder in my voice.

"Did *you* see that?" she asked, with the focus of the inquiry upon me. While I was enrapt in the ecstasy of sound and love from the mountain, she was watching the show from behind me. She reported that images of gold were entering my back in the darkness as I meditated. Drawings, charts, graphs, and schematics were entering me at the rate of about one every five or six seconds. She could remember any details of the golden plates, because they were complex and full of details, and they were entering at a rate too quickly to be memorized. She had never seen anything quite this. I certainly had no idea of what she was talking about, but I believed her because I felt like I had been filled with information of some kind. The most remarkable thing about her observation was that while this was occurring, she noticed my countenance change to one of deep peace. She placed her hand upon my deltoid area of my arm while the group sat quietly around us in the low-lighted room.

Over her hand she noticed another hand, golden in color and much illuminated. She found this so amazing that she moved her hand slightly, only to notice that within a second or so that the golden hand followed hers. As if trying the observation, she moved her hand a few times back and forth in a smoothing motion. The golden hand moved in a trailing motion to match hers. Supposing that she was herself having her first OBE, she decided it would be neat to leave the room and visit her sister in Michigan more than a thousand miles away. She made it as far as the ceiling of the house and felt like she slammed into the hard surface, after which the *golden one* said, "This is not about you, it is about him. Go back and observe and remember." Obeying the command, she did just that.

We talked quietly for about an hour as we all recounted what had happened, but I don't remember what was said. I was in a state of change. We have spoken about that night many dozens of times, and more details are continuously coming out. In fact, this book is the result of the *download* received that life-changing evening at the home of James Gilliland.

I went to sleep in the bed with the window facing Mount Adams. Sleep came easily, and the hour of seven AM arrived almost instantly. I arose, dressed, and headed to the downstairs bathroom for a shower. This bathroom was adjacent to the kitchen. As I headed for the shower with my toothbrush and towel in hand, Jonathan Shalomar was there washing dishes in the sink. I looked at him and said, "I feel different."

He looked at me for a moment with genuine discernment and said, "You *look* different." He studied me for a moment and asked me what happened. I recounted the events of the night before, and he said that this was typical for the Mount Adams ECETI ranch.

I took my shower and got ready for the day. As this was one of the largest conference events on the West coast, great opportunities existed to meet some of the best and greatest minds in the industry. Angelika Whitecliff was a speaker at the Earth Transformation Conference at the ECETI ranch that weekend as well. I went to speak to her.

I found her at her display booth in the main hall, wherein I repeated the events of the previous night. They were still fresh on my mind, and the effects were becoming quite amazing. She told me this was common for people when they get to a place and time where the purpose and information pertinent to a person were provided in one giant *download*. I had never heard of this word outside of computer language.

"What does that mean?" I asked.

"A *download* is where pure knowledge is poured into a person in order to meet a special need. I think your expedition to the North Pole to seek the opening into the inner Earth requires special knowledge. You got it in the form of a download last night." The explanation was clear enough, but I still had no idea what was going on.

"I am a scientist," I began. "I am used to taking measurements and gathering information with instruments, not with my body. This is a very weird feeling." I was so full of joy inside that the tears flowed easily. I am not one to cry easily either.

She continued, "When you get up there, and the captain of the ship has gone everywhere over the Arctic Sea you have predetermined to sail, you may find nothing. The captain is going to turn to you and say, 'Where to now Dr. Agnew?', and you will know where to go."

I was speechless. Yes, I had joined a team of scientists earlier that year to travel by ship to the Arctic region to seek such an opening, but I was only a contributing scientist. I was on the team to design a way to measure the curvature of the Earth so as to locate the legendary oceanic depression. I wasn't a key player. I was just on the team led by Steven Currey, who was an accomplished expedition leader with decades of experience in these types of adventures.

There was something else. My body was changing. I was an asthmatic since I was 5 years old, weighed 252 pounds, and had been taking hypertension medication for nearly 10 years. Just so you won't forget, I want to tell you I felt differently. I moved differently. When I returned again the next year to speak, the film manager approached me during dinner and said, "Your older brother was here last year speaking. I don't know what happened to you, but you look 15 years younger than the guy who was here speaking last year."

It was true. I watched the film of that lecture myself. That guy was older than me. I had undergone a metamorphosis during that download of information. When I returned home the following day, there were other things that happened. I was still reeling inside form the body and soul changes that had taken place. I phoned Rodney, my contact person with the Expedition, the first chance I had. His words were so surprising that I still recall the vacuous feeling as he said them. "I don't know if we're going to have an expedition," he began.

"Why?" I asked.

"Because Steven Currey died unexpectedly. Brain tumor. No one knew he was even sick. We don't know what to do," he said with a voice controlled to hide the emotion he was feeling.

I was inspired to tell Rodney what had happened over the weekend with the short version. "I'll call you back," he said and hung up.

The next day he called. He informed me that the expedition leadership board had met and decided to ask me to be the expedition leader. I was floored. Five days before, I was a hobby member with a shot at being on a team of explorers to the Arctic Circle. Now I was the expedition leader. Now I knew what Angelika meant. Now I knew what my mission was going to be.

The next three years prepared me for the greatest expedition in the history of the world. That, of course, is another story. The human race was pulsing with new found communication and was vibrating like it was about to bond in a spontaneous motion of love and entanglement. It needed an event to unite it. A planet and the souls upon her felt that this event had the potential to bring them together like a single being, without war and without loss of identity in a way that eased the patriotic sovereignty responsible for so much death and mayhem. The knowledge that we have always existed, and that we are the creators of this universe, was enough for the race to begin the next phase of evolution. We were all about to grow…again.

With *The Ark of Millions of Years* trilogy in the your hands (available also in audio) and *Remembering the Future*, I feel sure that these pages will leave you with the knowledge to make your lives more full of hope and excitement for your dreams and for your ability to love others.

Remember, it does not matter so much how you are loved. It matters how you love others. Even Jesus has enemies. The music and aroma of life has been created by you with all its stench and beauty. The pain and cold of birth, the joy and glory of falling in love, and the probability of physical death have all been your creation.

Sleeping souls are affecting the universe too, but without the empowerment that you now possess. I want you to awaken and discover that the separation you have perceived is also your creation. With this book, you are empowered to uncreate that separation from Source and build something new and amazing. When the real birthing pains arrive to Earth, it won't matter how many cars you own, or how large and diverse your 401k might be. In fact, like the great ones who have come to Earth and managed to be heard, you will see that possessions are not the goal of life. You are not separate from God. You do not need anyone to make the call for you. You are integral to God, like an essential organ. There are those who feel disconnected from *source*.

Now that you realize that the Big Bang never happened and that you cannot ever be separated from God, go and help someone else to realize the same thing. They feel that their lives are full of destiny and not under their control. Well, you feel differently now.

You know that you are not only in total control of your own life, but that your attention and intention do affect the universe in a very powerful way. You know how to dream. If you have read all the books in our series, you know the messages left for us by the ancient races that once lived here. They were and are us. We built those things to remind ourselves to wonder about them. That wonder reconnects us to our own past existences. You now know that the pyramids, the Nazca fields, the calendars, and the cosmos themselves were created by you to remind you of who you are. You were there. Search your heart. You know this is true.

You have worked for many thousands of years, perhaps millions of years to get to this point. You stand on the edge of the precipice along with the entire race of sentient beings on this planet, and you are no longer afraid. No one can place slices of fear and trepidation on your pizza. The waves of change are exactly why you came here.

Never stop loving and seeking love. Fall in love as deeply and thoroughly as you can. Savor the aroma, memorize the feel, and taste everything in moderation. These opportunities only come around during mortal experiences. It's the most exciting event in this corner of the universe, which after all is just a singularity anyway. We want you to walk away from the eschatological path whereby the human race is annihilated. You have the right and the power and now have the tools to change everything. So you might as well get to it. Above all else, remember the future.

Peace, Love and Joy.

The author will appear anywhere, anytime for a signing or lecturing event. Please contact me today at brooksagnew@yahoo.com to request an appearance at your local event. Book Clubs can speak directly to me by phone teleconference arrangements.

Table of Illustrations

Index